Facing mother
nature's wrath

Natural Disasters
Throughout
History

A Skill-Based Reading Anthology

Editorial Director: Susan C. Thies
Editor: Paula J. Reece
Contributing Writer: Sarah Beth Cavanah
Book Design: Jann Williams
Production: Nancy Suits
Photo Research: Lisa Lorimor

For information, contact
Perfection Learning® Corporation
1000 North Second Avenue, P.O. Box 500
Logan, Iowa 51546-0500.
Phone: 800-831-4190 • Fax: 800-543-2745
perfectionlearning.com

ISBN 0-7891-5888-4
Printed in the U.S.A.
1 2 3 4 5 6 PP 07 06 05 04 03 02

contents

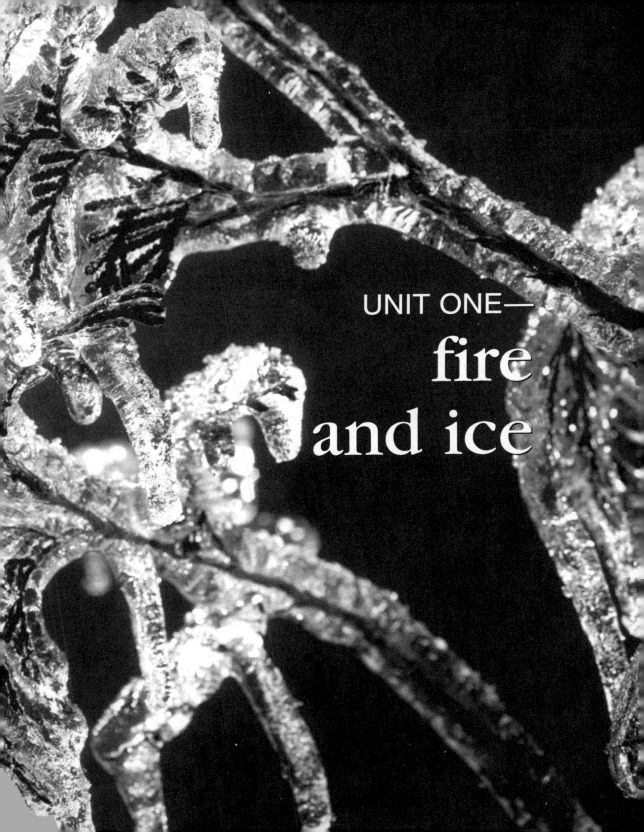

UNIT ONE—
fire
and ice

The Fire That Rebuilt Chicago

Sarah Beth Cavanah

Poor Mrs. O'Leary's cow. For more than 100 years, Mrs. O'Leary's cow has been blamed for the worst fire ever to strike an American city. It's possible Old Bessie did start the Great Chicago Fire of 1871, but maybe she didn't. Either way, Mrs. O'Leary's cow may have started a fire that saved a city.

One Big Tinderbox

[2]Today, Chicago is a great, modern midwestern city. But in 1871, it was the great western city. The Civil War had ended just six years earlier. Most Americans still lived in the eastern half of the United States and called everything west of the Missouri River the Wild, Wild West.

[3]Like the cities of the East, Chicago was a crowded, teeming city. Many Chicagoans were German and Scandinavian immigrants who worked for small wages in hard and sometimes dangerous jobs. People lived in crowded, wooden buildings, most of which didn't even have any space between them. Automobiles wouldn't become popular for 50 years, so people had to share their space with horses in wooden stables filled with dry hay. Electricity was also in the future. Fireplaces and oil lamps were used for warmth and light.

[4]Combine the wooden houses and stables with lots of hay and flames from fireplaces and lamps and you get a recipe for fire. Even the roads in Chicago were covered with wood. In fact, fires happened all the time in Chicago. Just the day before the Great Chicago Fire started on October 8, half of the city's 185 firefighters put out a large fire in the west part of the city. But no one expected the fire that was to come.

The Tinderbox Erupts

[5]It is true that the fire started in Mrs. O'Leary's barn. Later, the story would spread that Mrs. O'Leary's cow kicked over a lantern the widow had left in her barn. But no one really knows. Mrs. O'Leary's cow has been judged guilty with no proof.

[6]At first, the fire wasn't unusual at all. Mrs. O'Leary's barn was about a mile away from the center of downtown Chicago. It was easy for the fire watchman to spot the fire. At that time, one person was always at the top of a tall tower looking for fires. This could save precious time for firefighters, since there were no telephones. The watchman could tell the firefighters about any fires he saw.

[7]After the big fire the day before, everyone was tired. The watchman accidentally called the wrong firehouse to go to the wrong place. This wasted valuable time. While the firefighters went to the wrong building, the fire spread. Once the situation was sorted out, the tired firefighters didn't move quickly enough.

[8]Most people around the fire weren't scared. One man was told the fire was coming. He said he didn't care unless his own house was on fire. "There is a fire every Monday and Thursday in Chicago!" he said.

[9]But people soon started to realize that this fire was not like other fires. In just two hours the fire had become uncontrollable.

Escaping the Flames

[10]The fire was unstoppable. The people of Chicago went from ignoring the fire to being afraid it would kill them. They ran from their homes as fast as they could. Mothers and fathers carried small children. Others carried expensive property they didn't want to leave for the fire.

[11]All together, they raced down the streets hoping to escape the fire. But the fire was chasing them. At times, it was moving as fast as a person could run. The smoke and fire also made it hard to see. People trying to escape couldn't see in front of them. They also couldn't see the sky.

[12]As the fire grew larger, it also became more violent. A stiff wind was blowing. This spread the fire faster and gave it more fuel. Not that the fire needed any more fuel.

[13]The energy from the wood buildings was already making the fire into a giant, flaming tornado. Flames spun around as they raced

up the street. Pieces of buildings were sent flying toward the people running away.

[14]Not everyone was running. Some people saw the fire as a great opportunity to steal. No one was guarding the stores. So some people broke through the windows and doors and carried off everything they could. No one knows how much was stolen. But there were several reports of carriages traveling down the road with burning boxes onboard.

[15]Where could the people go? The fire was burning as fast as they could run. They would have just moments to rest before they had to begin running again. They couldn't run forever, but they couldn't stop either. Water seemed to be the only solution.

[16]There were two options for water: the Chicago River and Lake Michigan. Many people chose to cross the Chicago River. They thought the fire wouldn't be able to cross the river. But they were wrong.

10

The fire crossed bridges just as the people had done.

[17]Others decided to wade into the cold waters of Lake Michigan. They would be safe from the fire but would be trapped in the lake until it was gone. Most of these people stayed in the lake for hours.

[18]That night, the fire grew so large and so bright that people in the next state could see it. Chicago's firefighters kept trying to control the flames. But after a long, hard night, the city's waterworks burned down at 7:00 on Monday morning. Without any water to fight the fire, the firefighters gave up.

[19]All that could save Chicago now was rain. Finally, late on Monday night, rain started to fall. By 3 a.m. on Tuesday, the fires were out. It was 30 hours after the fire had started in Mrs. O'Leary's barn.

Chicago Comes Back Better

[20]Three hundred people died in the fire. But more than 17,000 buildings were destroyed. The fire had consumed everything in a four-mile by one-mile area. Stores, hotels, the baseball park, the courthouse, the post office, and most of Chicago's banks were gone. Approximately 100,000 people were homeless. These people made up one-third of the total population of Chicago. And winter was coming.

[21]As Americans heard what had happened in Chicago, they started sending money to help. Cities as large as New York City and as small as Lafayette, Indiana, gave money to help rebuild Chicago. One Chicagoan said it was "the grandest display of true Christian feeling the world ever saw. Here we were, hundreds of thousands of people—houseless, homeless, without food or shelter. And first from all parts of the United States, and then from every country and city in the civilized world, money came pouring in till in less than a fortnight we had to telegraph them to stop."

[22]Not everybody wanted to help, though. Southern cities thought the fire was God's revenge for the Civil War. During the war just six years earlier, a Northern general had ordered the city of Atlanta, Georgia, burned to the ground. Some thought it was only fair that Chicago had burned. And they were not shy about saying so.

[23]Unfortunately, some of the money didn't make it to the neediest people. A group of businessmen decided they would be in charge of giving out the relief money. They

agreed it shouldn't spoil the people of Chicago. So they would only let people who had jobs get a portion of the money. But many people had lost their homes and their jobs. When they couldn't prove they were working, they were forced to go hungry for lack of food.

[24]However, the fire wasn't all bad news. Suddenly, Chicago had the opportunity to rebuild its downtown area. Before, downtown had been full of twisting streets and strange arrangements of businesses, homes, and farms. When Chicago rebuilt, it made its downtown completely modern. Architects even found a new way to get the most out of expensive land. They bought little pieces and built up. Chicago soon became the world's capital for skyscrapers.

[25]Businesses were able to become more modern too. Most people moved into houses away from the downtown area. This left all the land open for business use. No one had to worry about any more cows kicking lanterns, either. All the farms moved outside the city too.

[26]Just one year after the horrible fire, people in Chicago were asking whether it had been a blessing in disguise. Many people had suffered and died, but the old, dangerous Chicago had been replaced by a truly modern city. Where there had been barns and crowded tenements, now there were better roads and safer buildings.

[27]We'll probably never know what started the Great Chicago Fire. But before you start blaming Mrs. O'Leary's cow, maybe you should thank her instead.

If you have been timing your reading speed for this story, record your time below.

_____ : _____
Minutes   **Seconds**

UNDERSTANDING THE MAIN IDEA

The following questions will demonstrate your understanding of what the story is about, or the *main idea*. Choose the best answer for each question.

1. This story is mainly about

Ⓐ why cities aren't made out of wood.

Ⓑ how a terrible fire gave Chicago the chance to become a better city.

Ⓒ how all the people of Chicago survived a terrible fire.

Ⓓ how some people in Chicago kept others from getting relief money.

2. This story could have been titled

Ⓐ "Burning Down and Building Up."

Ⓑ "The Life and Times of Mrs. O'Leary's Cow."

Ⓒ "Rain Finally Falls."

Ⓓ "Destruction of a Truly Modern City."

3. Which detail best supports the main idea of this story?

Ⓐ Many Chicagoans were German and Scandinavian immigrants.

Ⓑ Many people had died, but the old, dangerous Chicago had been replaced by a truly modern city.

Ⓒ Some people broke through windows and doors.

Ⓓ Some Southern people thought the fire was God's revenge for the Civil War.

4. Find another detail that supports the main idea of this story. Write it on the lines below.

_____

_____

RECALLING FACTS

The following questions will test how well you remember the facts in the story you just read. Choose the best answer for each question.

1. The Great Chicago Fire started in

Ⓐ the outskirts of town.

Ⓑ Mrs. O'Leary's barn.

Ⓒ Chicago's baseball stadium.

Ⓓ the train station.

2. Some people took advantage of the fire to

Ⓐ win the Civil War.

Ⓑ take a swim in Lake Michigan.

Ⓒ steal from unguarded stores.

Ⓓ build campfires.

3. The fire was finally put out by

Ⓐ rain.

Ⓑ Chicago's firefighters.

Ⓒ a snowstorm.

Ⓓ firefighters from around the country.

4. When people in other cities heard about Chicago's fire, they

Ⓐ banned farms from inside city limits.

Ⓑ sent the people of Chicago food.

Ⓒ moved to Chicago to help rebuild the city.

Ⓓ sent money to help the people of Chicago.

READING BETWEEN THE LINES

An *inference* is a conclusion drawn from facts. A *generalization* is a general statement, idea, or rule that is supported by facts. Analyze the story by choosing the best answer to each question below.

1. **What conclusion can you draw from paragraph 3?**

   Ⓐ Chicago was the first city in America to get electricity.

   Ⓑ Everyone in Chicago owned a horse.

   Ⓒ Automobiles had been invented, but not many people owned them.

   Ⓓ Most people in Chicago spoke German.

2. **What conclusion can you draw from paragraph 8?**

   Ⓐ Firefighters set fires every Monday and Thursday in Chicago.

   Ⓑ Chicagoans were braver than most Americans.

   Ⓒ The man wanted his house to burn down.

   Ⓓ The man wasn't scared because fires were common in Chicago.

3. **What generalization can you make from this story?**

   Ⓐ City fires can cause mass destruction.

   Ⓑ All Americans loved Chicago.

   Ⓒ Cows are always getting into trouble.

   Ⓓ Relief money is always given out fairly.

4. **What can you infer about Chicago from the story? Answer on the lines below, using complete sentences.**

   _____

   _____

   _____

   _____

   _____

DETERMINING CAUSE AND EFFECT

Choose the best answers for the following questions to show the relationship between what happened in the story (*effects*) and why those things happened (*causes*).

1. Because Chicago had so much wood, hay, and flames from lamps,

Ⓐ people had to live in crowded apartment buildings.

Ⓑ fires started all the time in the city.

Ⓒ automobiles weren't allowed in the city.

Ⓓ people called Chicago a great western city.

2. What happened because a stiff wind was blowing during the fire?

Ⓐ The fire became bigger from the extra fuel.

Ⓑ The wind blew the fire out.

Ⓒ The fire changed direction and crossed the Chicago River.

Ⓓ The fire became smaller, and many people were saved.

3. Why did the firefighters give up on Monday morning?

Ⓐ They had already put the fire out.

Ⓑ They were too tired to fight the fire any longer.

Ⓒ They didn't have any water to fight the fire after the waterworks burned down.

Ⓓ There were no more buildings left to save in the city.

4. Why did Southerners think the fire was God's revenge for the Civil War?

Ⓐ Chicago sent many soldiers to fight in the war.

Ⓑ A Southerner had started the fire.

Ⓒ A Northern general had burned the city of Atlanta, Georgia, during the war.

Ⓓ The fire started on the same day as the end of the Civil War.

USING CONTEXT CLUES

Skilled readers often find the meaning of unfamiliar words by using *context clues*. This means they study the way the words are used in the text. Use the context clues in the excerpts below to determine the meaning of each **bold-faced** word. Then choose the answer that best matches the meaning of the word.

1. "Like the cities of the east, Chicago was a crowded, **teeming** city."

CLUE: "People lived in crowded, wooden buildings, most of which didn't even have any space between them."

   Ⓐ open

   Ⓑ lazy

   Ⓒ calm

   Ⓓ full

2. "All together, they **raced** down the streets hoping to escape the fire."

CLUE: "They ran from their homes as fast as they could."

   Ⓐ played

   Ⓑ competed

   Ⓒ walked

   Ⓓ hurried

3. "Others decided to **wade** into the cold waters of Lake Michigan."

CLUE: "They would be safe from the fire but would be trapped in the lake until it was gone."

   Ⓐ wiggle

   Ⓑ enter

   Ⓒ wait

   Ⓓ wail

4. "One Chicagoan said it was 'the grandest **display** of true Christian feeling the world ever saw.' "

CLUE: "Cities as large as New York City and as small as Lafayette, Indiana, gave money to help rebuild Chicago."

   Ⓐ distance

   Ⓑ bank

   Ⓒ show

   Ⓓ poster

LESSON 2

The Armistice Day Blizzard of 1940

Mary Turck

The National Weather Service defines a blizzard as a snowstorm with winds of at least 35 miles per hour. The temperature falls to 20 degrees Fahrenheit or lower over the time of the storm.

[2]During a blizzard, snow or blowing snow makes it impossible to see farther than one quarter of a mile. And the snowstorm must last at least three hours.

[3]A severe blizzard has winds of 45 miles per hour or more. These winds blow snow, and temperatures drop to 10 degrees or lower.

[4]The word *blizzard* was first used to describe a snowstorm in an Iowa newspaper in the 1870s. Before that time, blizzard was used to describe rounds of gunfire during a battle. One root word of blizzard is the German word *blitz*, which means "lightning."

Unexpected Weather

[5]Howard Turck was a senior in high school at the time of the Armistice Day blizzard. He remembers getting on the bus that warm, calm morning with no hat or gloves.

[6]Twenty minutes after the bus picked up Howard, the skies grew dark and the wind began to blow. Soon, neither the students nor the driver could see the road. Then the bus slid into a ditch at the side of the gravel road.

[7]About half an hour later, the bus driver asked some of the bigger boys to go for help. Howard and three other seniors volunteered. Howard got a stocking cap from one of the girls. Two of his pals borrowed hats or caps too. Gene Shaw, the fourth volunteer, thought he would be fine without one.

[8]The four teenagers got off the bus and started looking for help. The howling wind and snow were blinding. The boys couldn't see the telephone poles at the side of the road. In fact, they couldn't see the road itself!

[9]Slowly, they made their way. They followed the road by feeling the gravel under their feet.

[10]After the four had gone a little way, they came to a stalled car. Howard and the other three crouched behind the car. There, sheltered from the wind, they tried to catch their breath. Then they pushed on through the storm.

[11]When the swirling snow let up for a moment, the boys saw a grove of trees and a farmhouse. A girl welcomed them and let them in to thaw out.

[12]By now, all four boys agreed that Gene needed a cap. The girl said her dad had just died. She offered Gene her father's cap. But Gene was afraid to wear a dead man's cap.

[13]Howard wasn't afraid, so he gave Gene his borrowed stocking cap. Then Howard put on the dead man's hat, and the boys set out for town again.

[14]Out of breath and energy, the boys were lucky once more. This time, the four found a stalled buttermilk truck. No one was in the truck. The boys stayed behind it long enough to catch their breath and recover their energy.

[15]After resting, the four pushed toward town—half a mile, one mile, a mile and a half, two miles.

[16]Finally, the boys reached the first house at the edge of town. The man of the house said he would drive the four boys to school. They all piled into his Model-T and rode the final half mile.

[17]At school, the teens told the principal that the bus was stuck in

the ditch. The storm didn't look so bad in town. So the principal said he would loan the boys skis, and they could ski home.

[18]"We told him he was nuts," Howard remembers. "We told him you couldn't see anything outside town."

[19]The boys convinced the principal that they could not go home on skis. So they found places to stay in town.

[20]"We would never have made it if we hadn't had [that car] and that buttermilk truck to hide behind so we could catch our breath," says Howard. "You couldn't see anything along the road. Not even the phone poles. Nothing at all. Just the gravel under your feet."

[21]But what happened to the kids back on the bus? The next day, the storm let up a little. The four boys decided to find their friends.

[22]The man who owned the lumberyard had a big team of horses. Each horse weighed between 1,200 and 1,400 pounds. He and the four boys gathered all the football parkas from school. Then they hitched the big horses to a sled and set out.

[23]Huge snowdrifts had formed where the boys had pushed through blowing snow the day before. As heavy as the horses were, they could still walk right over the top of the hard-packed drifts, pulling the sled behind them.

[24]The rescue team found that the other kids had walked half a mile to a farmhouse. Some were frostbitten. Their hands and cheeks had frozen as they walked through the storm.

[25]They had stayed at the farmhouse overnight. They were glad to see the four senior boys, the sled, and the team. The horses hauled all the kids back to town. It was three days before their parents could get into town to take them home.

Back on the Farm

[26]"When we got back home," recalls Howard, "we found out that 20 of our neighbors' cows had frozen to death. They froze standing straight up in the field."

[27]Many other cows were caught out in the storm. Some were frozen stiff and dead where they stood. Others were blinded by ice that had formed on their heads. Or they had suffocated when their breath had frozen into ice and covered their nostrils.

[28]Some cows lost their hair. Icy blizzard winds blew the cows' hair

straight out from their bodies. Snow caught around the hair, freezing into icy chunks that pulled the hair out.

[29]When the blizzard hit, farmers went to look for their animals. "Horses," said one survivor of the blizzard, "had 'storm smarts.' They found shelter near trees or buildings."

[30]Howard's father had gone out when the storm started to look for his horses. "He couldn't see them," Howard recalls. "So he walked back toward the grove and hollered for them. They came after 15 or 20 minutes and stood by the barn until he let them in."

[31]Another farm family rescued near-frozen cattle from the pasture. They tied the cattle's feet and dragged them, one at a time. They took them back to the barn that was half a mile away.

[32]The cattle had been lying, near frozen, on the ground. By the time they got back to the barn, some had recovered enough to attack their helpers! But still only 17 of the 28 rescued cows survived the blizzard.

[33]Many chickens, turkeys, and geese froze to death during the storm. Some survived, even though they had been buried under the snow.

[34]At Howard's farm, a hen and eight or ten chicks were buried in some brush in a snowdrift. They stayed there, snug and safe. It was two or three days before the family found them and dug them out!

[35]Sheep had a harder time. A teenage boy at Backus, Minnesota, went with his father to look for their 15 sheep. They found the sheep frozen tight to the ground. The sheep could not get up! So the boy and his father broke them loose from the ice and hauled them into the barn. Those sheep were lucky!

Coping with the Blizzard

[36]One young bride was at home on the farm alone on the day after the Armistice Day blizzard. Her husband never got back from his town job. The young wife knew she had to milk the cow and feed and water the horses.

[37]But when the young bride opened the door, she couldn't get out. The whole door was blocked by a giant snowdrift. She finally climbed out through a window and set to work.

[38]After taking care of the animals, she dug a tunnel back to the house. Although she was a city girl, this young woman made a good farmer. She knew that she had to take care of the animals that depended on her.

[39]People in the city had blizzard stories too. Many people were trapped downtown by the blizzard.

[40]Dayton's department store reserved a whole floor of one hotel for its employees. A government employee caught downtown in the storm felt that her office was too cold. So she went to the jail and slept there overnight!

[41]Many people were trapped in streetcars overnight. One man walked a mile to his home after his car went off the road. When he got there, he just walked out of his frozen coat. It stood on the floor by itself!

[42]Even in the days after the blizzard, getting around town was difficult. Roads were blocked by stalled and buried cars. Some cars were buried so deep that they could not be seen. People used poles to poke through the snow, trying to locate their buried cars.

[43]Streetcars were buried to their tops in the snow. They had to be dug out and the lines cleared before they could run again. Some doctors went on skis to visit sick patients in the days following the storm.

If you have been timing your reading speed for this story, record your time below.

_____ : _____

Minutes   **Seconds**

UNDERSTANDING THE MAIN IDEA

The following questions will demonstrate your understanding of what the story is about, or the *main idea*. Choose the best answer for each question.

1. This story is mainly about

Ⓐ how a war ended with a blizzard.

Ⓑ how people survived when a blizzard hit their town.

Ⓒ how people took care of their animals during a blizzard.

Ⓓ how some chickens survived when they were buried with snow.

2. This story could have been titled

Ⓐ "Snowstorm."

Ⓑ "Rainstorm."

Ⓒ "Windstorm."

Ⓓ "Winter Begins."

3. Which detail best supports the main idea of this story?

Ⓐ A severe blizzard has winds of 45 miles per hour or more.

Ⓑ The young wife knew she had to milk the cow and feed the horses.

Ⓒ The boys stayed behind the buttermilk truck long enough to catch their breaths and recover their energy.

Ⓓ Some cows lost their hair.

4. Find another detail that supports the main idea of this story. Write it on the lines below.

_____

_____

RECALLING FACTS

The following questions will test how well you remember the facts in the story you just read. Choose the best answer for each question.

1. Before the 1870s, *blizzard* was used to describe

Ⓐ mild snowstorms.

Ⓑ an ice cream dish.

Ⓒ terrible rainstorms.

Ⓓ rounds of gunfire.

2. Gene wouldn't wear the hat the girl in the farmhouse had because he

Ⓐ didn't think it was cold enough to wear a hat.

Ⓑ was afraid to wear a dead man's hat.

Ⓒ didn't like the color of the hat.

Ⓓ didn't want to owe the girl anything.

3. When the teenage boys went back to the school bus, they found out that

_____

_____

_____

4. In Backus, the boy and his father had to

Ⓐ hook their horses up to a sled.

Ⓑ dig a tunnel back to their house.

Ⓒ hide in a buttermilk truck.

Ⓓ break their sheep loose from the ice.

Facing Mother Nature's Wrath

READING BETWEEN THE LINES

An *inference* is a conclusion drawn from facts. A *generalization* is a general statement, idea, or rule that is supported by facts. Analyze the story by choosing the best answer to each question below.

1. What conclusion can you draw from paragraph 5?

Ⓐ Howard didn't usually take the bus to school.

Ⓑ Howard didn't think students should have to go to school on Armistice Day.

Ⓒ Howard had lost his hat and gloves.

Ⓓ When he got on the bus, Howard didn't know that a storm was coming.

2. What conclusion can you draw from paragraph 14?

Ⓐ The driver of the buttermilk truck had left it days ago.

Ⓑ The driver of the buttermilk truck was waiting in the truck.

Ⓒ The driver of the buttermilk truck had left on foot.

Ⓓ The driver of the buttermilk truck had died.

3. What generalization can you make from this story?

Ⓐ No one has ever died in a blizzard.

Ⓑ Blizzards are dangerous.

Ⓒ It always snows on Armistice Day.

Ⓓ Being a farmer is very hard work.

4. It can be inferred from the story that the children's parents

Ⓐ didn't care what happened to their children.

Ⓑ had to wait three days to get them because they couldn't get through the snow.

Ⓒ were told they would have to wait three days before they could get their children.

Ⓓ thought their children were having fun at the farmhouse.

———— ■ ————

DETERMINING CAUSE AND EFFECT

Choose the best answers for the following questions to show the relationship between what happened in the story (*effects*) and why those things happened (*causes*).

1. Because the bus driver couldn't see the road,

Ⓐ he turned the bus around.

Ⓑ he called the principal to say they wouldn't make it in.

Ⓒ Howard took the dead man's hat and gave his hat to Gene.

Ⓓ the bus slid into a ditch on the side of the road.

2. What happened because the storm didn't look as bad in town?

Ⓐ The principal decided not to go after the kids in the bus.

Ⓑ The boys decided to head back to the bus right away.

Ⓒ The principal told the boys to ski home.

Ⓓ Horses found shelter near trees or buildings.

3. Why did some cows lose their hair?

Ⓐ The people had to cut it to make coats.

Ⓑ The cows scratched it off on trees.

Ⓒ Snow got caught in the hair, causing it to get pulled out.

Ⓓ The people had to shave the cows to help treat them for frostbite.

4. Why did the young bride climb out the window?

Ⓐ She didn't want any snow to get inside the house.

Ⓑ She couldn't get out the door because a snowdrift was blocking it.

Ⓒ She didn't want to scare the animals.

Ⓓ She was from the city and wasn't a very good farmer.

———■———

Facing Mother Nature's Wrath

USING CONTEXT CLUES

Skilled readers often find the meaning of unfamiliar words by using *context clues*. This means they study the way the words are used in the text. Use the context clues in the excerpts below to determine the meaning of each **bold-faced** word. Then choose the answer that best matches the meaning of the word.

1. "Howard and three other seniors **volunteered**."

CLUE: "The four teenagers got off the bus and started looking for help."

  Ⓐ refused

  Ⓑ deserted

  Ⓒ offered

  Ⓓ evacuated

2. "When the **swirling** snow let up for a moment, the boys saw a grove of trees and a farmhouse."

CLUE: "The howling wind and snow were blinding."

  Ⓐ blowing

  Ⓑ wet

  Ⓒ warm

  Ⓓ still

3. "The boys stayed behind it [the truck] long enough to catch their breath and **recover** their energy."

CLUE: "After resting, the four pushed toward town . . ."

  Ⓐ remove

  Ⓑ redo

  Ⓒ uncover

  Ⓓ regain

4. "They [the chickens] stayed there, **snug** and safe."

CLUE: "At Howard's farm, a hen and eight or ten chicks were buried in some brush in a snowdrift."

  Ⓐ comfortable

  Ⓑ sleepy

  Ⓒ dangerous

  Ⓓ sneaky

———————■———————

Avalanche at Snowstorm Peak

Jane Duden

Jack Ritter did not know that Sunday, November 17, 1985, would be his last day alive. Lester Morlang had no idea about the disaster ahead. The men were at their gold mine, the Bessey G. It was high in the Colorado mountains.

[2]The mine had two portals. One was on the west side of the mountain. But the men were at the east portal. There were no roads on this side and no people for miles.

[3]It was nearly 6 p.m. A blizzard was brewing. Snowstorm Peak loomed above. Its slopes were heavy with snow.

[4]This was avalanche country. An avalanche is a crashing, sudden river of snow. But the miners thought they'd have warning. They could duck inside the mine.

[5]The men switched on the lights on their miner's hats. They were building a roof over the old east portal. The roof would keep snow away. Jack ran a small diesel-powered loader on treads. Lester stood in the bucket. The loader lifted the bucket to roof level. Lester put a timber into place. Then— *avalanche!* The men never saw or heard it coming. And so began the struggle to survive.

Buried Alive!

[6]The avalanche began right at the mine. Suddenly megatons of snow covered Jack. It flipped Lester out of the bucket and buried him. The snow sped on down the canyon. It ran over anything in its path.

[7]Lester's body was locked under tons of snow. He knew he must dig out or he would die in a tomb of ice. Is this what it's like to die? he thought in panic.

[8]Lester was buried with his hands in front of his face. That was lucky. His hands formed a tiny air pocket. Wiggling his fingers made more space to breathe. Could he dig out more space ahead?

[9]He could hear the loader running. He called to Jack. But yelling made him lose his breath. So Lester made himself breathe slowly. This kept him from inhaling the light, feathery snow.

[10]Lester thought about his wife and son. He sent thoughts to his dad, asking for help. He prayed. He made up his mind to live.

[11]He grabbed a fistful of snow and pulled it toward his chest. Then he grabbed another, and another. Straining every muscle, he pushed with his elbows. He moved ahead a few inches!

[12]On he dug. After a while, the loader quit. Now there was dead silence. Sick with fear, Lester hoped Jack was safe. Maybe Jack had dug back in the mine and gone for help. But who could help them? There was nobody for miles.

[13]Lester clawed at the snow. He wriggled like a caterpillar. Cramps twisted his stomach. His hands were frozen. His muscles hurt. He rested. Then he clawed some more.

[14]Ten hours passed, and then 15. The lamp on Lester's miner's hat still shone. He saw only an endless white blank. Without the light, everything went black. He thought of his family. He would NOT give up!

Still Trapped

[15]Then, after 22 hours, Lester turned off his lamp again. And this time he saw light! It was now about 4:00 on Monday afternoon. He soon broke his way to freedom, leaping with joy. Lester Morlang had dug through 30 feet of snow!

[16]But Lester's ordeal was not over. His hands were numb. It was freezing outside. A blizzard was raging. And it would soon be dark. He was still trapped on the mountain.

[17]Lester tried to stamp out HELP in the snow. But the wind blew snow over the letters. He used his hard hat for a scoop to make the end of the tunnel into a snow cave. He huddled inside for the night.

[18]Meanwhile, the sheriff was just getting the news. Jack Ritter's son had found the mine's east portal blocked with snow. He had seen no sign of his dad or Lester Morlang. The sheriff's heart sank. Most buried avalanche victims are alive after

15 minutes. After 30 minutes, less than half are alive. By now, a day had passed. Outside, a blizzard blew fiercely. No one could get there tonight. The search would have to wait until daylight.

[19]In his snow cave, Lester waited. He jammed his frozen hands into his armpits. During the night, a second avalanche came. But the snow raced over the top of the cave. Scared to death, Lester counted. He thought about his family. He prayed for all he was worth.

The Search

[20]At daybreak Tuesday, the rescue effort began. Strong winds drove the wind chill to 50 degrees below zero. A helicopter flew over the mine. The crew flew low. They looked for clues—a hat, a boot, a glove. But all they saw was snow. If only they could land at the east portal. But it was too steep and windy.

[21]There was danger of another avalanche. So the pilot got permission to make the snow stable. That meant setting off bombs. The bombs started thundering rivers of snow. Now the slopes were safe for rescuers to search.

[22]Powerful snowplows started up the roads. Another helicopter brought searchers. One was Lester's father. He awoke in the night, thinking that he heard Lester calling to him, telling him he was cold. Mr. Morlang felt certain that his son was alive.

[23]The helicopter landed at the west portal. The searchers waded through the mine's long tunnel. Then they came out the east portal. Shoveling into the snow, they soon found Jack Ritter. His frozen body lay by the loader.

Facing Mother Nature's Wrath

Down the Mountain

[24]Lester was again digging out. He knew he had to follow the mine safety plan. Get down to Junction Creek. Go to the first farmhouse.

[25]Lester heard a roaring in the sky. It was a helicopter! He waved frantically. But it did not see him. It sped beyond the ridge, up to the mine.

[26]Then Lester heard the explosions. He knew they were meant to start avalanches. Lester was right in the path! He scrambled behind a big tree. The tree kept the rumbling snow away. When it was over, Lester stepped out onto new hard-packed snow. It was 15 to 20 feet deep. He was angry, but the rescue team had no way of knowing he was down there.

[27]He had to keep going. Sliding and falling, Lester went forward. The snow was like concrete. If the avalanche had carried him down there, he could never have dug out. At last, Lester reached the bottom of the avalanche path. Now he faced deep powder snow. He had to pack the snow five or six times just to take each step. If he didn't, he'd sink to his chest in snow.

[28]Lester tells the rest of the story. "Just before dark, the searchers took one more run. This time they flew over the path of our safety plan. The sheriff knew the plan.

[29]"I was already past the hard pack and back into the soft snow. I heard the 'copter. I held up my hands. They saw me!

[30]"The ravine was narrow. Not much wider than the 'copter blades. I knew at any time the next avalanche would come. The 'copter hovered. I climbed up on a big snow-covered rock. The pilot came down close enough so I could grab the skid on the helicopter. I was hanging on with my elbow. When I jumped on, the engine stalled in the narrow, tight spot. I yelled, 'Go, go, go!' They got me inside. They told me, 'You're a miracle!' "

The Miracle Man of Snowstorm Peak

[31]"I'd seen plenty of avalanches," says Lester. "I never really was scared of them. Today I still ride snowmobiles. But I know a good place and a bad place. Jack Ritter was wise about that. We were pushing it. We knew it was going to avalanche again on that old side of the mine. We were building that little porch overhang so the snow would run off it.

[32]"After the avalanche, I talked to a lot of experts. You have to know the type of snow, the time of day. You can tell where an avalanche is going to be. They have their paths through the year.

[33]"I feel really lucky. I lost only the tip of one finger. I couldn't walk for a long time. I was in bed for weeks. My feet were numb. It took a year of therapy. I had to learn how to get my balance and how to walk again. The love and support of [my family] helped the months go faster.

[34]"We've always been a tight family. But the avalanche made everything tighter. Some days I just stop and remember. Then just the simplest thing can be so grand."

[35]Lester is no longer a miner. He owns gravel trucks and does custom hauling. He put up a memorial for his partner at the mine. And he named the west portal after Jack Ritter—*The J. R. Portal*. As for Lester, he is the Miracle Man of Snowstorm Peak.

If you have been timing your reading speed for this story, record your time below.

_____ : _____

Minutes   ***Seconds***

Facing Mother Nature's Wrath

UNDERSTANDING THE MAIN IDEA

The following questions will demonstrate your understanding of what the story is about, or the *main idea*. Choose the best answer for each question.

1. This story is mainly about

Ⓐ how a man climbed to the top of Snowstorm Peak.

Ⓑ how a man survived a snowstorm only to die in a helicopter crash.

Ⓒ how two friends survived an avalanche together.

Ⓓ how a man survived an avalanche.

2. This story could have been titled

Ⓐ "Jack's Survival Tale."

Ⓑ "The Miracle Man of Snowstorm Peak."

Ⓒ "Friendship Saves the Day."

Ⓓ "The Death of Lester."

3. Which detail best supports the main idea of this story?

Ⓐ Jack Ritter didn't know he would die on that Sunday.

Ⓑ Only one-half of avalanche victims survive more than 30 minutes.

Ⓒ The sheriff's heart sank.

Ⓓ Lester turned a tiny air pocket in the snow into an escape tunnel.

4. Find another detail that supports the main idea of this story. Write it on the lines below.

_____

_____

RECALLING FACTS

The following questions will test how well you remember the facts in the story you just read. Choose the best answer for each question.

1. On Sunday, November 17, 1985, Jack and Lester were

Ⓐ fighting a snowstorm to get home.

Ⓑ at their gold mine in the Colorado mountains.

Ⓒ in their homes asleep.

Ⓓ at a ski resort in the Virginia mountains.

2. To catch the attention of rescuers, Lester

Ⓐ started a bonfire.

Ⓑ made a trail with his hat and boots.

Ⓒ tried to stamp out HELP in the snow.

Ⓓ climbed to the top of a tall tree.

3. To make the snow more stable for rescuers, the pilot asked to

_____

_____

_____

4. Lester named the west portal of the mine

Ⓐ The Miracle Portal.

Ⓑ The J. R. Portal.

Ⓒ The Jack Portal.

Ⓓ The No Escape Portal.

READING BETWEEN THE LINES

An *inference* is a conclusion drawn from facts. A *generalization* is a general statement, idea, or rule that is supported by facts. Analyze the story by choosing the best answer to each question below.

1. **What conclusion can you draw from paragraph 4?**

   Ⓐ Avalanches usually don't give much warning.

   Ⓑ Jack and Lester knew an avalanche was coming.

   Ⓒ Avalanches were uncommon in this area.

   Ⓓ Avalanches happened often in this area.

2. **What conclusion can you draw from paragraph 16?**

   Ⓐ Lester was afraid of the dark.

   Ⓑ Lester was imagining that he had dug his way out of the snow.

   Ⓒ Lester knew he could be home in just an hour.

   Ⓓ It still wasn't certain that Lester would survive.

3. **What generalization can you make from this story?**

   Ⓐ Rescuers always give up looking for survivors one day after an avalanche.

   Ⓑ Very few people could survive as long as Lester did in the snow.

   Ⓒ No one survives an avalanche.

   Ⓓ Good friends never make good business partners.

4. **It can be inferred from the story that**

   Ⓐ Jack didn't have the will to survive that Lester did.

   Ⓑ Lester's father had survived an avalanche when he was younger.

   Ⓒ Lester could have saved Jack.

   Ⓓ Lester's experience made him look at life differently.

Facing Mother Nature's Wrath

DETERMINING CAUSE AND EFFECT

Choose the best answers for the following questions to show the relationship between what happened in the story (*effects*) and why those things happened (*causes*).

1. **Because Lester's hands were buried in front of his face, he**

    Ⓐ couldn't dig out of the snow.

    Ⓑ could see which way to dig.

    Ⓒ wasn't able to move at all.

    Ⓓ had an air pocket from which to breathe.

2. **What happened because Lester yelled after being buried?**

    Ⓐ Jack called back to him.

    Ⓑ Lester knew he was close to the surface.

    Ⓒ The rescuers could tell where Lester was.

    Ⓓ Lester began losing his breath.

3. **Why didn't the helicopter land at the east portal?**

    Ⓐ The rescuers didn't know anyone was in the mine.

    Ⓑ It was too steep and windy.

    Ⓒ The rescuers knew Jack and Lester were at the west end.

    Ⓓ The pilot could see Lester running down the mountain.

4. **Why did Lester have to pack the snow five or six times before he took each step?**

    Ⓐ He was following an old mining superstition.

    Ⓑ He was trying to make a trail the rescuers could see.

    Ⓒ If he didn't, he would sink up to his chest in snow.

    Ⓓ His legs were so cold, he couldn't move without making small moves.

USING CONTEXT CLUES

Skilled readers often find the meaning of unfamiliar words by using *context clues*. This means they study the way the words are used in the text. Use the context clues in the excerpts below to determine the meaning of each **bold-faced** word. Then choose the answer that best matches the meaning of the word.

1. "The mine had two **portals**."

CLUE: "They were building a roof over the old east portal."

  Ⓐ passages

  Ⓑ staircases

  Ⓒ entrances

  Ⓓ loaders

2. "Now there was **dead** silence."

CLUE: "He [Lester] could hear the loader running."

  Ⓐ almost

  Ⓑ deceased

  Ⓒ total

  Ⓓ late

3. "He [Lester] **scrambled** behind a big tree."

CLUE: "Lester was right in the path [of the avalanche]!"

  Ⓐ stirred

  Ⓑ ran

  Ⓒ walked

  Ⓓ mixed up

4. " 'We've always been a **tight** family,' he [Lester said]."

CLUE: " 'The love and support of [my family] helped the months go faster.' "

  Ⓐ close

  Ⓑ loose

  Ⓒ hard

  Ⓓ tense

Facing Mother Nature's Wrath

Fire in Yellowstone Sparks Fires in Minds

Sarah Beth Cavanah

In 1988, Yellowstone National Park was ablaze. Over the summer, around one-third of the Greater Yellowstone Ecosystem would be consumed by the fire. By the time winter snows finally put out the last flames, more than 25,000 firefighters would have worked on the fire. Two firefighters were killed. But all this action was nothing compared to the debate surrounding the great fire.

Natural Experiment

[2]Yellowstone was the first national park in the United States. Its beauty and wonders caused President Theodore Roosevelt to declare that Yellowstone would be left in its natural state. For more than 100 years, Americans have come to Yellowstone to see attractions such as Old Faithful, a geyser that erupts on a regular hourly schedule. People have also come to see animals like bison, elk, and grizzly bears that have disappeared from other places.

[3]Over time, other wildlife areas around Yellowstone were given national protection as well. Today, Yellowstone is part of the Greater Yellowstone Ecosystem. This is a large area of protected areas that includes Yellowstone, Grand Teton National Park, and a few national forests. Because Yellowstone was the very first national park, it held a special place in America's heart.

[4]For quite a bit of Yellowstone's history, the people who worked for the National Park Service would put out any fires they found. Their job was to protect the park, so they didn't want fire to harm it.

[5]But science was learning more about how complex natural systems

really were. After decades of putting out all fires, park officials were noticing that the forests were changing.

[6]When you think of a forest, you probably see lots of tall trees that block out the sun. But there are all kinds of forests. Entire forests can have an age, just like an animal or a single plant. Old forests have very big trees. These trees block sunlight from getting to the ground. Since most plants need sunlight to live, not much grows underneath the trees. These forests give homes and food to many different types of animals.

[7]There are also young forests that have a mixture of all sorts of plants. There are young trees called saplings. Plus, there are lots of flowers, bushes, and vines. Many different types of animals live in these types of forests as well. Scientists say these areas have biodiversity, meaning they have many different types of plants and animals.

[8]You can find baby forests too, but you might not think of them as forests. Baby forests don't have trees you can see. They usually look like meadows filled with grass and flowers. Many animals also live in these places.

[9]Even though forests age like animals, they don't die in the same way. Trees can live for a very long time. Some trees can live to be thousands of years old. Old trees don't have any predators, except for people. So nothing eats them when they die. Instead, a dead tree can keep standing long after it dies. After many years, it might fall down. Then it can take hundreds of years for bacteria and fungus to break a tree down into soil.

[10]An old forest has to die to make way for a baby forest. Yellowstone's forests were old. So were forests in other national parks. Scientists decided that nature had a way of getting old forests out of the way—fire. It was a big breakthrough in thinking about conservation. Fire and destruction were necessary to keep a forest healthy. Park caretakers started letting fires burn.

The Fire
[11]The fires of 1988 seemed as if they would be like all the other fires, at least for a while. Park officials waited for the small fires that had started early in the summer to go out on their own. But no rain fell. So the fires kept growing. By August, 80 fires were burning. Officials decided to try to put out all the fires before the entire area burned.

[12]This was a huge job. On windy days, a fire could travel more than ten miles. Features of the landscape that normally stopped fires weren't working. The fire jumped a huge river canyon.

[13]Firefighters tried their own ways to stop the fire. They dug large trenches, hoping to stop the flames. They burned old, dead trees in small fires. They thought they could keep the old, dry trees from adding fuel to the big fires. Firefighting pilots dropped water and chemicals from low-flying planes to try to kill the flames.

[14]The firefighters' efforts were working, but not well enough to stop the flames. It was hard, dangerous work. Plus, there weren't enough firefighters. Members of the National Guard and other military personnel were sent to help. Two people were killed in the fires, and both were firefighters. One was battling flames on the ground, while another was flying a plane.

[15]Scientists weren't even sure the firefighters should be trying. They thought the fire would be good for the park. And even if it wasn't, it didn't look like the firefighters could stop the fire.

[16]But scientists aren't the only people who care about the park. Many people in the area make a living off the tourists who come to visit the park. These people were worried that they wouldn't be able to make enough money if fire destroyed the park.

[17]Many people also owned ranches around the park. They were worried that fire couldn't read a property map. If the fire inside the park couldn't be controlled, then it could easily move on to private property. There it would burn valuable rangeland and cattle herds.

[18]As the fires became larger, they also started to make the news. People all across the country saw television footage of Yellowstone burning. They didn't want to see the nation's first park destroyed. And they weren't hearing how the fire could help the park. Americans knew that if you wanted to save a house from fire, you stopped it. They thought the same way about the fires in Yellowstone. Many called their elected officials and asked them to have the fires stopped.

[19]Everyone was getting very upset. In the end, it was up to nature to stop the fires. Despite everything the firefighters did, it was the winter snows that put out the last of the fires. But just because the fire was out, it didn't mean the anger was over.

The End and the Beginning

[20]The government called hearings to decide who was responsible for the Yellowstone fires. President George Bush declared that now all fires in national parks would be put out, whether or not they started naturally. The American public was saddened when they saw pictures of the blackened land that had once been green forests.

[21]Things were not as bad as they seemed. One-third of the Yellowstone ecosystem had been burned by the fires, but most of the land had been spared. After the winter snows melted in spring, green returned to Yellowstone. Some areas were still blackened, but park officials were excited to see rare plants taking advantage of the newly opened land.

[22]Scientists discovered that the old forests were much more likely to be destroyed. Filled with old, dead trees, these parts of the forest were filled with fuel for the fires. The fires hadn't burned in straight lines. Instead, they burned in a patchwork-quilt pattern. Next to destroyed areas were young forests that had gone untouched.

[23]John Varley, the park's chief scientist, discovered how the fire could be a good thing for plants. In all his years in Yellowstone, Varley had never seen mountain hollyhock. "I've been here 20 years, and I've never seen a single one," he said. But then, one day, Varley was out hiking and saw an amazing sight. "There was a hillside covered with their lavender blooms—so many of them it was too thick to walk through." If the fire hadn't cleared trees away, the mountain hollyhock would not have been able to bloom in such numbers.

[24]The fire was also good for trees. Many lodgepole pines were destroyed in the fire. But it also helped new pines start. Lodgepole pines need temperatures of over 113 degrees Fahrenheit to open their cones. They need a fire to spread their seeds. Without it, new trees can't get started.

[25]Fears about how the fire would affect animals were also worse than the truth. Scientists were worried that the fire would rob rare species like grizzly bears and bison of their food supply. They were very surprised when large animal numbers went up after the fire. Instead of taking away food supplies, it opened up new areas to animals.

[26]The fire also brought more tourists to Yellowstone. Many people who had visited the park before the fire came back to see the difference.

This helped the local businesses who had worried tourists would never return after the fires.

Long Way to Go

[27]It will take a century for the signs of the fire to completely disappear. Saplings that got their start from the fire will need hundreds of years to match the size of trees that were destroyed. The trenches firefighters were forced to build will take even longer to recover.

[28]The Yellowstone fires taught Americans a lot about fire's role in nature. The park service has gone back to letting fires burn if they are naturally created. It hasn't always worked out for the best. But no one can deny that fires have a place in our national parks. Sometimes destruction is necessary for creation to begin.

If you have been timing your reading speed for this story, record your time below.

_____ : _____

Minutes   *Seconds*

UNDERSTANDING THE MAIN IDEA

The following questions will demonstrate your understanding of what the story is about, or the *main idea*. Choose the best answer for each question.

1. This story is mainly about

Ⓐ how firefighters beat a huge fire in Yellowstone Park.

Ⓑ how fires destroy forests forever.

Ⓒ how Yellowstone Park was destroyed by fire.

Ⓓ how a fire in Yellowstone Park caused a debate on park rules.

2. This story could have been titled

Ⓐ "To Burn or Not to Burn."

Ⓑ "Fire Claims Hundreds of Lives."

Ⓒ "No More Fires in Yellowstone."

Ⓓ "The Death of Yellowstone."

3. Which detail best supports the main idea of this story?

Ⓐ Yellowstone is part of the Greater Yellowstone Ecosystem.

Ⓑ Trees can grow for a very long time.

Ⓒ On windy days, a fire could travel more than ten miles.

Ⓓ Many people called their elected officials and asked them to have the fires stopped.

4. Find another detail that supports the main idea of this story. Write it on the lines below.

_____

_____

RECALLING FACTS

The following questions will test how well you remember the facts in the story you just read. Choose the best answer for each question.

1. Yellowstone Park was the first

Ⓐ park to catch on fire.

Ⓑ national park.

Ⓒ tourist attraction in the United States.

Ⓓ amusement park.

2. Baby forests look like

Ⓐ meadows.

Ⓑ old forests.

Ⓒ tall trees.

Ⓓ black hills.

3. Scientists thought the fires

Ⓐ should be put out immediately.

Ⓑ should be allowed to burn.

Ⓒ were too big for just firefighters to fight.

Ⓓ were destroying baby forests.

4. The Yellowstone fires burned

Ⓐ in a straight line.

Ⓑ the entire park.

Ⓒ all the towns around the park.

Ⓓ in a patchwork-quilt pattern.

Facing Mother Nature's Wrath

READING BETWEEN THE LINES

An *inference* is a conclusion drawn from facts. A *generalization* is a general statement, idea, or rule that is supported by facts. Analyze the story by choosing the best answer to each question below.

1. What conclusion can you draw from paragraph 5?

Ⓐ Natural systems are really very simple.

Ⓑ The forests were changing because more people lived in them.

Ⓒ Someone was starting fires on purpose.

Ⓓ The forests were changing because there had been no fires.

2. What conclusion can you draw from paragraph 11?

Ⓐ A lot of rain fell in the summer of 1988.

Ⓑ Park officials had started the fires.

Ⓒ Rain usually puts out natural fires.

Ⓓ By August, there weren't many fires to worry about.

3. What generalization can you make from this story?

Ⓐ People all over the United States cared about Yellowstone Park.

Ⓑ Fires are always bad for forests.

Ⓒ Yellowstone Park will never recover from the fires of 1988.

Ⓓ All forests look alike.

4. It can be inferred from the story that people wanted the fires stopped because

_____

_____

_____

_____

_____

—■—

DETERMINING CAUSE AND EFFECT

Choose the best answers for the following questions to show the relationship between what happened in the story (*effects*) and why those things happened (*causes*).

1. Because Yellowstone was the very first national park,

   Ⓐ it held a special place in America's heart.

   Ⓑ no fires were allowed to burn in the park.

   Ⓒ fires weren't allowed to be put out in the park.

   Ⓓ no one cared if it was destroyed by fire.

2. What happened because there weren't enough firefighters?

   Ⓐ National Guard and other military personnel were asked to help.

   Ⓑ They were forced to give up trying to put out the fires.

   Ⓒ The fires destroyed the entire park.

   Ⓓ The firefighters had to concentrate on just a few small fires.

3. Why did the people who made a living off visitors to the park want the fires stopped?

   Ⓐ They thought the fire would burn down their shops.

   Ⓑ They didn't want baby forests.

   Ⓒ They thought people would stop coming to visit if the park were destroyed.

   Ⓓ They wanted the firefighters to leave.

4. Why did the lodgepole pines need the fire?

   Ⓐ Fire got rid of other trees around the pines.

   Ⓑ They were all too old to grow anymore.

   Ⓒ The mountain hollyhock were killing them.

   Ⓓ Fire is the only way they can spread their seeds.

———■———

Facing Mother Nature's Wrath

USING CONTEXT CLUES

Skilled readers often find the meaning of unfamiliar words by using *context clues*. This means they study the way the words are used in the text. Use the context clues in the excerpts below to determine the meaning of each **bold-faced** word. Then choose the answer that best matches the meaning of the word.

1. "In 1988, Yellowstone National Park was **ablaze**."

CLUE: "Over the summer, around one-third of the Greater Yellowstone Ecosystem would be consumed by the fire."

   Ⓐ on fire

   Ⓑ cold

   Ⓒ angry

   Ⓓ destroyed

2. "The fire **jumped** a huge river canyon."

CLUE: "Features of the landscape that normally stopped fires weren't working."

   Ⓐ stopped

   Ⓑ destroyed

   Ⓒ crossed

   Ⓓ made

3. "The government called hearings to decide who was **responsible** for the Yellowstone fires."

CLUE: "But just because the fire was out, it didn't mean the anger was over."

   Ⓐ remembered

   Ⓑ needed

   Ⓒ required

   Ⓓ to blame

4. "The Yellowstone fires taught Americans a lot about fire's **role** in nature."

CLUE: "But no one can deny that fires have a place in our national parks."

   Ⓐ characters

   Ⓑ part

   Ⓒ evilness

   Ⓓ home

End-of-Unit Activities

1. **In order to survive a disaster, people must make decisions that they hope will save their lives. Choose three disasters from this unit. For each disaster, analyze a decision that was made by filling in the chart below. Then decide which decision you think had the largest impact on its particular disaster. On the lines below the chart, justify your answer with facts from the stories.**

	Disaster 1:	Disaster 2:	Disaster 3:
Decision Made			
Person Who Made Decision			
Consequence of Decision			
Impact Decision Had on Disaster			

_____

_____

_____

_____

_____

Facing Mother Nature's Wrath

End-of-Unit Activities

2. **Rank each of the stories in this unit, from the one you liked the most to the one you liked the least. For each story, write one interesting fact you learned. Then write a paragraph describing why you liked the story you ranked *1* the best.**

LESSON 1 Ranking _____

_____

_____

_____

LESSON 2 Ranking _____

_____

_____

_____

LESSON 3 Ranking _____

_____

_____

_____

LESSON 4 Ranking _____

_____

_____

_____

Why did you like the story you ranked *1* the best?

_____

_____

_____

_____

Words-Per-Minute Chart

Directions:

Use the chart to find your words-per-minute reading speed. Refer to the reading time you recorded at the end of each article. Find your reading time in seconds along the left-hand side of the chart or minutes and seconds along the right-hand side of the chart. Your words-per-minute score will be listed next to the time in the column below the appropriate lesson number.

No. of Words	Lesson 1 1,464	Lesson 2 1,543	Lesson 3 1,498	Lesson 4 1,515	Minutes and Seconds
80	1,098	1,157	1,124	1,136	1:20
100	878	926	899	909	1:40
120	732	772	749	758	2:00
140	627	661	642	649	2:20
160	549	579	562	568	2:40
180	488	514	499	505	3:00
200	439	463	449	455	3:20
220	399	421	409	413	3:40
240	366	386	375	379	4:00
260	338	356	346	350	4:20
280	314	331	321	325	4:40
300	293	309	300	303	5:00
320	275	289	281	284	5:20
340	258	272	264	267	5:40
360	244	257	250	253	6:00
380	231	244	237	239	6:20
400	220	231	225	227	6:40
420	209	220	214	216	7:00
440	200	210	204	207	7:20
460	191	201	195	198	7:40
480	183	193	187	189	8:00
500	176	185	180	182	8:20
520	169	178	173	175	8:40
540	163	171	166	168	9:00
560	157	165	161	162	9:20
580	151	160	155	157	9:40
600	146	154	150	152	10:00
620	142	149	145	147	10:20
640	137	145	140	142	10:40
660	133	140	136	138	11:00
680	129	136	132	134	11:20
700	125	132	128	130	11:40
720	122	129	125	126	12:00
740	119	125	121	123	12:20
760	116	122	118	120	12:40
780	113	119	115	117	13:00
800	110	116	112	114	13:20
820	107	113	110	111	13:40
840	105	110	107	108	14:00

Seconds (left side) / *Minutes and Seconds* (right side)

Facing Mother Nature's Wrath

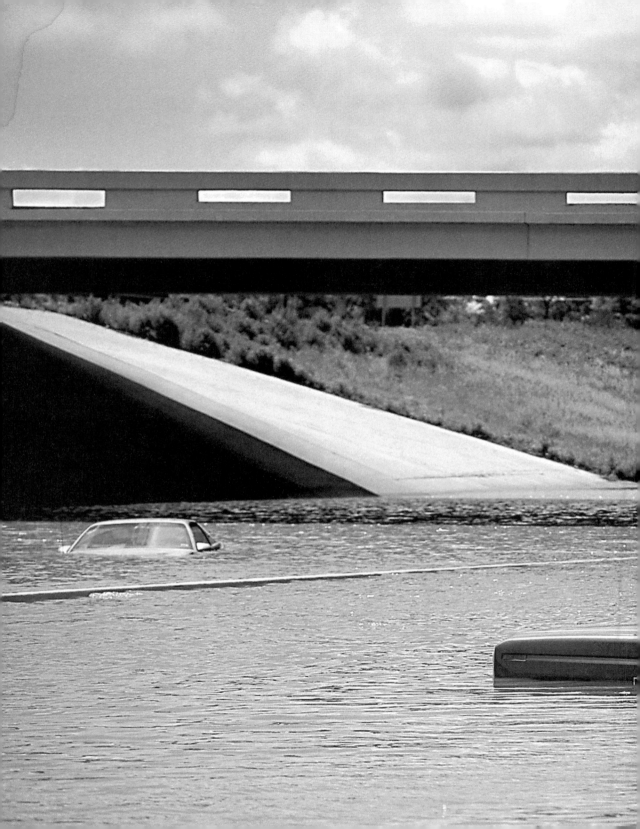

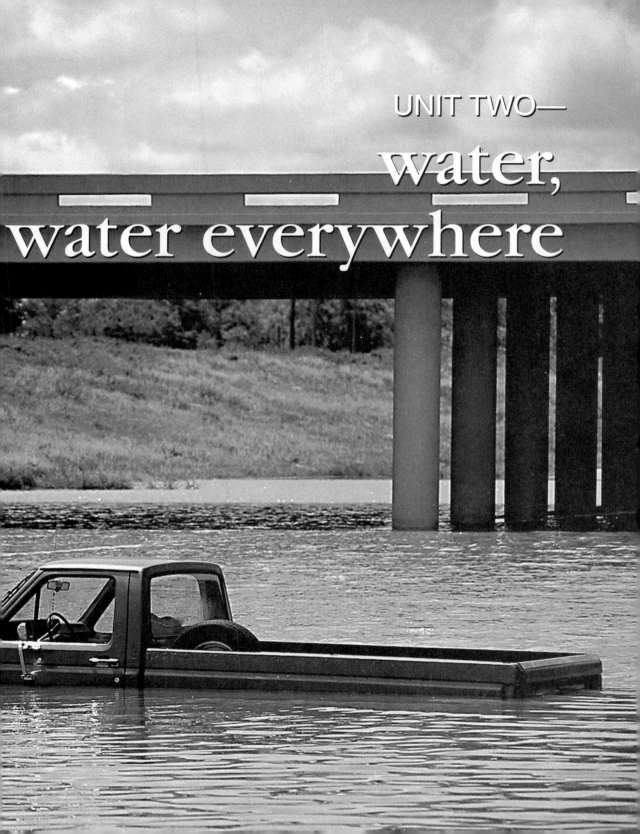

water, water everywhere

The Johnstown Flood

Sarah Beth Cavanah

[1]The South Fork Hunting and Fishing Club was thought to be the best place to spend the summer. All the richest and most famous people in Pittsburgh, Pennsylvania, were members. Everyone loved the club.

[2]But all that ended on May 31, 1889. The dam that held back the artificial lake the club was built on burst. A wall of water 40 feet high and traveling 40 miles per hour raced down the valley to the nearest community, Johnstown. Before the day was over, 2,209 people were dead.

[3]Every survivor of the Johnstown flood lost someone they loved. The government and the members of the South Fork Hunting and Fishing Club told the grieving families that the flood had been an act of God. But many people didn't think so. They thought the flood wasn't a natural disaster. They thought the South Fork Club was to blame.

Two Different Worlds

[4]The South Fork Hunting and Fishing Club was a wonderful place. When the Pennsylvania Railroad was sold and no longer needed the dam on the Little Conemaugh River, members of the club bought it. They made it bigger and higher so it would hold back more water. By doing this, the club made a beautiful, two-mile by one-mile lake perfect for summertime use.

[5]On their lake, the club members built "small" cabins. (At least, they were small to the members. Many of the cabins had nearly 20 rooms!) They would sail ships on the lake, throw parties, and just have a good time.

[6]Johnstown was a much different place. The working-class people had

enough to eat and roofs over their heads. But they were poor in comparison to the super-rich members of the South Fork Hunting and Fishing Club. Most of the men worked in mines or steel mills. Married women stayed at home looking after their families, and some did washing and cleaning for richer families.

[7]Life in the two communities couldn't have been more different. But they shared one thing in common: the dam. And people on both sides knew the dam was in trouble.

The Dam Breaks

[8]Instead of hiring an engineer to rebuild the dam to make the lake, the club members had decided to save money. They had hired a man who built railroads and knew very little about dams. He made the dam bigger and stronger by shoving rocks, tree stumps, and dirt into holes in the old dam.

[9]Lots of people thought this was a bad idea. People in Johnstown complained about the dam all the time. They knew if it broke, the water would head straight for their homes.

[10]People in the club were worried too. By the last day of May in 1889, some of the members had

moved out there to spend the summer. They didn't like what they saw. It had been a very snowy winter and a very rainy spring. The dam was struggling to hold it all in.

[11]Some of the members made a last-ditch effort to make the dam stronger. But it was too late. Rain had been falling all night and most of the day. The dam broke. Now there was nothing anyone could do to stop the water or save Johnstown.

[12]"We've got to get out!"

[13]Six-year-old Elsie Schaffer was playing with her rag doll on the kitchen floor. Something was going on, but Elsie didn't know what. The adults were talking quickly about the river and the dam.

[14]Then Elsie heard something very strange. It was a train whistle. But instead of a few short little toots of the horn, the whistle was screaming in one long burst. The train's engineer was trying to warn people that something terrible was coming.

[15]Elsie's father, John, burst into the house. "The dam is broken!" he yelled. "We've got to get out!"

[16]John grabbed Elsie and her older sister, while Elsie's mother went to get the sleeping baby. They rushed out of the house and uphill toward Elsie's grandmother's home.

[17]They could hear the water racing toward them. It was 40 feet tall and going 40 miles per hour. Elsie held tight to her father. They were in a race against death.

[18]The water was coming closer and closer. It looked as if the Schaffer family wouldn't reach high enough ground in time.

[19]But Elsie's parents didn't stop. The water was nearly to them. With all the energy they could, the family raced on.

[20]They made it! Elsie and her family watched as just feet below them, the top of the wall of water rushed by.

[21]Elsie was safe, but the water went on. Just two miles downriver, another six-year-old girl was in its path.

"Throw That Baby!"

[22]Gertrude Quinn didn't make it to high land in time. Instead, the girl found herself hanging on to a mattress as the water swept her away.

[23]Gertrude was all alone. A roof with 20 people on it floated by. Gertrude called out for the people to save her. No one did anything. The people on the roof were holding on for dear life, and Gertrude was too far away.

[24]But then Gertrude saw a man moving toward the edge of the roof. The people on the roof tried to stop the man, but he broke free from them. He plunged into the quickly moving waters and disappeared.

[25]The man's head came up out of the water. Gertrude called to him. She begged him to save her. The man started swimming toward Gertrude. Then he disappeared into the water. By that time, it was 20 feet deep.

[26]Just as Gertrude was starting to think the man had drowned, his head reappeared, much closer to her. But then he was gone again.

[27]Gertrude kept believing the man would appear again. Gertrude didn't know the man, but she knew in her heart that he would save her. Then the man's head came up, right next to Gertrude's raft-mattress.

[28]The man lifted Gertrude off the mattress. She wrapped her little arms around his neck and held on as tightly as she could. Together, Gertrude and the man went downstream with the flood. Gertrude could hear the crying and moaning of people caught in the waters. They were drowning, just like she would if they couldn't get out of the water.

[29]After a while, Gertrude saw two men inside a building that stood on

Facing Mother Nature's Wrath

a hill. The building was high enough and strong enough to have stood firm against the flow of the water. The men had poles and were using them to pull people out of the water. But Gertrude and her savior were too far out for the poles to reach.

[30] "Throw that baby over here to us!" one of the men called.

[31] "Do you think you can catch her?" Gertrude's hero asked.

[32] "We can try!"

[33] So Gertrude's savior threw her 15 feet. The men with the poles snatched her up and pulled her to safety.

[34] But her hero, a man she later found out was named Maxwell McAchren, kept going with the water.

Coffins Everywhere

[35] Finally, the lake ran out of water. The water level in Johnstown got lower and lower until the survivors could see the land again.

[36] But what they could see was horrible. Whole buildings had been picked up and stacked against hills like pieces of lumber. Roads were just piles of mud and sediment from the lake. And in the mud, thousands of dead bodies were partly buried.

[37] More than 2,000 people had died, including 99 entire families and 396 children under the age of ten. Those who survived were left with horrible memories. Seven-year-old Anna Bridges watched as a mother and her baby were swept under the waves. Anna Alberter, 16, watched as the schoolhouse floated down the street. It almost crashed into Anna's house when it suddenly turned and blocked the water, saving her whole family.

[38] But not everyone was so lucky. Six-year-old Mary Dillon's family had to swim out from their house. Mary's father told her sister to hold on to him. But a brick hit her in the head, and she was lost. In all, Mary lost 26 relatives in the flood.

[39]Elsie Schaffer's father did business in wood. Although it wasn't his normal business, John Schaffer turned his operation toward making coffins. Bodies were everywhere. Elsie was constantly surrounded by them. There just weren't enough people to perform all the funerals.

Natural Disaster?

[40]After the flood, things were much different at the South Fork Hunting and Fishing Club. Since all the cabins were upstream from the dam, they weren't hurt in the flood. Even so, all the members left by June 1. Their perfect summer resort was ruined. They went home.

[41]Volunteers came from all over the country to help the people of Johnstown. This disaster was the first one in which the Red Cross became involved. Reporters from all over the world came as well. The Johnstown Flood became the first real international news event.

[42]The reporters' stories inspired many Americans to send money to help the survivors. Johnstown was grateful to have it, but it wasn't enough.

[43]Many survivors thought the members of the South Fork Hunting and Fishing Club should help pay for the rebuilding of Johnstown. After all, they said, it was the club's dam that had caused the flood. Shouldn't the members be held responsible?

[44]Some survivors even went to court to try to get the club to pay for the disaster. But the courts said the flood was an act of God—something that couldn't be blamed on people.

[45]Johnstown did rebuild, but without help from the South Fork Hunting and Fishing Club. The town even flooded again, but nothing like the great flood of 1889.

> *If you have been timing your reading speed for this story, record your time below.*
>
> _____ : _____
>
> *Minutes   Seconds*

UNDERSTANDING THE MAIN IDEA

The following questions will demonstrate your understanding of what the story is about, or the *main idea*. Choose the best answer for each question.

1. This story is mainly about

Ⓐ a flood that destroyed a town and killed thousands of people.

Ⓑ how people in Johnstown complained about the dam.

Ⓒ how Elsie Schaffer and her family escaped the flood.

Ⓓ how the people of Johnstown tried to get the South Fork Hunting and Fishing Club to pay for the flood.

2. This story could have been titled

Ⓐ "A Beautiful Summer."

Ⓑ "A Lucky Day."

Ⓒ "A Broken Dam."

Ⓓ "A Hero's Tale."

3. Which detail best supports the main idea of this story?

Ⓐ Before the day was over, 2,209 people were dead.

Ⓑ The South Fork Hunting and Fishing Club was a wonderful place.

Ⓒ Johnstown even flooded again, but nothing like the great flood of 1889.

Ⓓ Elsie Schaffer's father did business in wood.

4. Find another detail that supports the main idea of this story. Write it on the lines below.

_____

_____

RECALLING FACTS

The following questions will test how well you remember the facts in the story you just read. Choose the best answer for each question.

1. On May 31, 1889,

Ⓐ Johnstown, Pennsylvania, was built.

Ⓑ the courts ruled the flood was an act of God.

Ⓒ the South Fork Hunting and Fishing Club's dam burst.

Ⓓ Gertrude Quinn turned six years old.

2. Elsie heard the train whistle

Ⓐ make one long alarm sound.

Ⓑ blow in short little bursts.

Ⓒ become silent.

Ⓓ blow in a long-short pattern.

3. The men Gertrude saw in the building were

Ⓐ watching people drown.

Ⓑ trying to rescue people with poles.

Ⓒ fighting over space on the roof.

Ⓓ crying.

4. Elsie Schaffer's father turned his wood business toward making

Ⓐ houses.

Ⓑ canes.

Ⓒ beds.

Ⓓ coffins.

READING BETWEEN THE LINES

An *inference* is a conclusion drawn from facts. A *generalization* is a general statement, idea, or rule that is supported by facts. Analyze the story by choosing the best answer to each question below.

1. **What conclusion can you draw from paragraph 5?**

   Ⓐ Cabins were larger in the 1800s than they are today.

   Ⓑ Twenty rooms isn't very many for a house.

   Ⓒ Members of the club spent most of the day working.

   Ⓓ The members of the club who built cabins were used to large houses.

2. **What conclusion can you draw from paragraph 22?**

   Ⓐ Gertrude was watching the flood from dry land.

   Ⓑ Gertrude was caught in the floodwaters.

   Ⓒ Gertrude's parents didn't try to save her.

   Ⓓ Gertrude's parents weren't home when the flood came.

3. **What generalization can you make from this story?**

   Ⓐ No one thought the dam would hold.

   Ⓑ Floods destroy many people's homes.

   Ⓒ Most people in Johnstown didn't know how to swim.

   Ⓓ Everyone in Johnstown missed the South Fork Hunting and Fishing Club.

4. **It can be inferred from the story that the South Fork Hunting and Fishing Club and the people of Johnstown**

   Ⓐ liked each other a lot.

   Ⓑ weren't good friends.

   Ⓒ shared many parts of their lives.

   Ⓓ lived very similar lives.

DETERMINING CAUSE AND EFFECT

Choose the best answers for the following questions to show the relationship between what happened in the story (*effects*) and why those things happened (*causes*).

1. Because it had been a very snowy winter and a very wet spring,

Ⓐ no one was coming to the South Fork Club.

Ⓑ the mines had to shut down.

Ⓒ the dam was struggling to hold all the water in.

Ⓓ school had been called off for the year.

2. What happened because Gertrude called out to the people on the roof?

Ⓐ She fell off her mattress.

Ⓑ Her parents were able to find her.

Ⓒ Her mattress hit dry ground.

Ⓓ A man jumped into the water to save her.

3. Why were the people Gertrude heard crying and moaning?

Ⓐ They were drowning in the water.

Ⓑ They were sad about all the people who had died.

Ⓒ They had painful injuries.

Ⓓ They were trying to get to Gertrude to help her.

4. Why did the flood end?

Ⓐ The dam was repaired.

Ⓑ The lake ran out of water.

Ⓒ The water was diverted to another valley.

Ⓓ The hot summer sun dried up the water.

USING CONTEXT CLUES

Skilled readers often find the meaning of unfamiliar words by using *context clues*. This means they study the way the words are used in the text. Use the context clues in the excerpts below to determine the meaning of each **bold-faced** word. Then choose the answer that best matches the meaning of the word.

1. "The dam that held back the **artificial** lake the club was built on burst."

CLUE: "By doing this, the club made a beautiful, two-mile by one-mile lake perfect for summertime use."

   Ⓐ natural
   Ⓑ manmade
   Ⓒ shallow
   Ⓓ dangerous

2. "The government and the members of the South Fork Hunting and Fishing Club told the **grieving** families that the flood had been an act of God."

CLUE: "Every survivor of the Johnstown flood lost someone they loved."

   Ⓐ excited
   Ⓑ giving
   Ⓒ saddened
   Ⓓ bored

3. "He **plunged** into the quickly moving waters and disappeared."

CLUE: "But then Gertrude saw a man moving toward the edge of the roof. The people on the roof tried to stop the man, but he broke free from them."

   Ⓐ stepped
   Ⓑ ran
   Ⓒ skipped
   Ⓓ jumped

4. "But Gertrude and her **savior** were too far out for the poles to reach." (paragraph 29)

Write what you think the **bold-faced** word means. Then record the context clues that led you to this definition.

Meaning:

_____

_____

_____

Context clues:

_____

_____

_____

—————■—————

The Hilo and Aleutian Tsunami

Sarah Beth Cavanah

Laura Chock woke up quickly. Something was wrong.

²The 18-year-old girl didn't take the time to put on clothes. She went downstairs to her parents' shop still wearing her pajamas.

³Laura knew many Americans thought she lived in paradise. But Hawaii could be as dangerous as it was beautiful. Less than five years before, the Japanese had bombed Pearl Harbor, Hawaii. Many people had died, and many American ships were destroyed. The bombing had caused the United States to join World War II.

⁴The war was supposed to be over. But what if it wasn't? What if the Japanese were back?

⁵But when Laura made it downstairs to the chicken shop, she didn't see fire and destruction from bombs. Instead, she found herself standing in water up to her knees. Laura and her family looked around. It wasn't the war, but it was still dangerous.

⁶Outside, children were playing in the flooded streets. They were screaming with delight. To them, the water seemed like a great new toy. They didn't know what was coming.

⁷Suddenly, a wave of water 5 feet high crashed through the doors and windows of the store. Laura and her family raced up the stairs. They avoided drowning, but the chickens in their cages weren't so lucky.

⁸Laura and her family waited for the water to go back down. Then they quickly ran downstairs and out into the street. The family was trying to move inland. They didn't want to be caught in another wave.

⁹Laura struggled to carry her five-year-old sister. Two more children

held on to her as they tried to move as quickly as they could through the knee-deep water. The strong tug of the water ripped off Laura's shoes and one of her pajama legs. But there was no time to stop.

[10]Laura noticed that the children were still screaming. But now they were screaming in fear.

[11]Finally, Laura and her family made it to dry and high ground. Many people stood in the street looking around at one another and down toward the shore. Children were asking their parents what had happened. The adults knew. It was a tsunami, a huge wave that destroys everything in its path.

[12]"Why didn't someone tell us it was coming?" a child asked. But the answer was that no one knew.

Birth of a Tsunami

[13]The tsunami that rushed through Laura's family's shop started thousands of miles away. It was just after midnight on April Fool's Day in 1946. An earthquake was shaking the ocean floor near the Aleutian Islands in the state of Alaska.

[14]Nature was playing an April Fool's Day joke. No one could feel an earthquake on the ocean floor. So how would they even know it happened?

[15]But this was no joke. Ocean earthquakes aren't dangerous for the shaking, but for what the shaking causes. The violent action of the earthquake pushes the water.

[16]Think about what happens when someone jumps into a swimming pool. The force from the body causes the water to move. After a while, the waves reach the far end of the pool. Not a big deal, right? Now imagine hundreds of people jumping into the pool at once. The force would be much stronger, causing the waves at the end of the pool to be much bigger as well. This is similar to what happens with a tsunami.

[17]Hawaii wasn't the only place to feel the force of the tsunami. On the Alaskan island of Unimak, five men lost their lives.

[18]The men were working at the Scotch Cap Lighthouse on the island. Their job was to warn ships in the dark to avoid the rocky areas around the island. But they didn't get enough warning about the tsunami headed their way.

[19]A wave nearly 100 feet high crashed into the lighthouse. It swept the men away and threw them onto the hard, rocky ground.

[20]Just like a person jumping into the middle of a pool, the wave

spread in all directions. Strangely, tsunamis are only dangerous to people on land. While out in the ocean, the tsunami is almost invisible.

[21]While at sea, the waves are only a few feet high and usually more than 100 miles apart. Ships sail right over the waves and airplanes flying over cannot see them. But the waves move quickly, 600 miles per hour or more.

[22]When the water gets shallower, the waves slow down. They start to grow larger and closer together. Six hours after the earthquake, waves traveling 30 miles an hour and 100 feet high crashed into Hilo, Hawaii.

No Warning

[23]Even though a tsunami had hit Alaska hours before, no one in Hawaii knew what was coming. James U. C. Low was driving in his car. When he looked toward the shore, he couldn't believe his eyes. A great wall of water was coming toward him from the bay. It was like nothing he had ever seen.

[24]James didn't know what to do. He drove toward a gas station. He thought he could take shelter inside. But by the time he got to the station, the wave had gotten to him. The water rushed through the windows and the joints in the car.

[25]James suddenly found himself neck-deep in water and frozen in fear. James might not have been moving, but his car was. The wave was pushing the whole car, with James in it. The spell was broken. James jumped out the window and escaped.

[26] The first wave hit as students and teachers at Laupahoehoe School were preparing to begin the day. Masuo Kino was outside the school when the wave hit. It picked him up and flipped him over.

[27] Masuo had no control. The wave was carrying him toward a rock wall that ran around the area of the school. Masuo thought, "I'm going to die. I'm going to hit headfirst into that rock wall, and I'm going to die."

[28] There was nothing Masuo could do. The water shot him toward the wall. Then, just before he hit, another part of the wave hit the wall. The wall collapsed and Masuo was saved. Instead of going headfirst into a solid wall, Masuo was pushed along with the pieces of the broken wall.

[29] Sixteen students and five teachers were killed at Laupahoehoe School. Overall, 159 Hawaiians died from the tsunami.

[30] No one wanted to be caught with no warning again. The American government developed a system to warn people that tsunamis were coming. They set up the Pacific Tsunami Warning System in Honolulu, Hawaii, to watch for events that could cause a tsunami. The center puts out "tsunami watches" that are like thunderstorm or tornado watches in mainland America.

[31] Laura's chicken shop survived the 1946 tsunami. It was later destroyed in another tsunami in 1960. But thanks to better warning, no tsunami in Hawaii has ever been as deadly as the one Laura survived in 1946.

If you have been timing your reading speed for this story, record your time below.

_____ : _____

Minutes   *Seconds*

Facing Mother Nature's Wrath

UNDERSTANDING THE MAIN IDEA

The following questions will demonstrate your understanding of what the story is about, or the *main idea*. Choose the best answer for each question.

1. This story is mainly about

Ⓐ how a chicken shop was destroyed.

Ⓑ how some lighthouse workers survived a disaster.

Ⓒ how a young boy survived a tsunami.

Ⓓ how a huge wave caused destruction in Hawaii and Alaska.

2. This story could have been titled

Ⓐ "Laura Loses Her Shoes."

Ⓑ "Wall of Water."

Ⓒ "Masuo Misses the Wall."

Ⓓ "Happy April Fool's Day!"

3. Which detail best supports the main idea of this story?

Ⓐ Laura didn't have time to put on clothes.

Ⓑ The tsunami took place on April Fool's Day.

Ⓒ Overall, 159 Hawaiians died in the tsunami.

Ⓓ Tsunamis are only dangerous to people on land.

4. Find another detail that supports the main idea of this story. Write it on the lines below.

_____

_____

RECALLING FACTS

The following questions will test how well you remember the facts in the story you just read. Choose the best answer for each question.

1. Five years before the tsunami,

Ⓐ the Japanese had bombed Pearl Harbor in Hawaii.

Ⓑ five men died at an Alaskan lighthouse.

Ⓒ the Laupahoehoe School had closed.

Ⓓ the Pacific Tsunami Warning System had been started.

2. The strong tug of the water

Ⓐ ripped off Laura's shoes and one of her pajama legs.

Ⓑ pulled Laura's sister away from her.

Ⓒ kept Laura from getting up the hill.

Ⓓ pulled Laura back to the chicken shop.

3. The men killed in Alaska worked for

Ⓐ the Irish Cap Restaurant.

Ⓑ the English Cap Fishery.

Ⓒ the Welsh Cap School.

Ⓓ the Scotch Cap Lighthouse.

4. Masuo Kino was picked up by the wave and pushed toward

Ⓐ a rock wall.

Ⓑ the ocean.

Ⓒ a chicken shop.

Ⓓ safety.

Facing Mother Nature's Wrath

READING BETWEEN THE LINES

An *inference* is a conclusion drawn from facts. A *generalization* is a general statement, idea, or rule that is supported by facts. Analyze the story by choosing the best answer to each question below.

1. What conclusion can you draw from paragraph 4?

Ⓐ Laura thought the war might have started again.

Ⓑ Laura was dreaming.

Ⓒ Laura's father had been killed in the war.

Ⓓ The Japanese had returned to attack Hawaii again.

2. What conclusion can you draw from paragraph 10?

Ⓐ The children were still playing in the water.

Ⓑ The children were now afraid of the water.

Ⓒ The children wanted to go back to their homes.

Ⓓ Laura was too scared to hear the children.

3. What generalization about tsunamis can you make from this story? Answer on the lines below, using complete sentences.

_____

_____

_____

_____

_____

4. It can be inferred from the story that the Tsunami Warning System

Ⓐ does not work.

Ⓑ is no longer used.

Ⓒ can stop tsunamis from hitting land.

Ⓓ has helped people survive tsunamis.

DETERMINING CAUSE AND EFFECT

Choose the best answers for the following questions to show the relationship between what happened in the story (*effects*) and why those things happened (*causes*).

1. Because Laura didn't have time to put on clothes, she

Ⓐ wasn't able to escape the wave.

Ⓑ went downstairs in her pajamas.

Ⓒ had to wait out the wave in her bedroom.

Ⓓ had to turn back during her escape.

2. What happened because there had been an earthquake in the ocean?

Ⓐ The tsunami was stopped.

Ⓑ Everyone was warned about the approaching tsunami.

Ⓒ A tsunami hit Alaska and Hawaii.

Ⓓ James U. C. Low was frozen in fear.

3. Why did the men in Alaska die?

Ⓐ The wave swept them from the lighthouse and onto the ground.

Ⓑ The lighthouse caught fire.

Ⓒ They drowned inside the lighthouse.

Ⓓ They were swept out to sea by the wave.

4. Why did Masuo not hit the wall?

Ⓐ He swam against the wave away from the wall.

Ⓑ One of the teachers pulled him out of the water in time.

Ⓒ Another part of the wave tore the wall down before he got there.

Ⓓ The wave stopped just before Masuo got to the wall.

———— ■ ————

USING CONTEXT CLUES

Skilled readers often find the meaning of unfamiliar words by using *context clues*. This means they study the way the words are used in the text. Use the context clues in the excerpts below to determine the meaning of each **bold-faced** word. Then choose the answer that best matches the meaning of the word.

1. "Laura knew many Americans thought she lived in **paradise**."

CLUE: "But Hawaii could be as dangerous as it was beautiful."

Ⓐ another country

Ⓑ the United States

Ⓒ the ocean

Ⓓ a wonderful place

2. "They [The children] were screaming with **delight**."

CLUE: "Outside, children were playing in the flooded streets."

Ⓐ joy

Ⓑ fear

Ⓒ damage

Ⓓ anger

3. "The wall **collapsed** and Masuo was saved."

CLUE: "Instead of going headfirst into a solid wall, Masuo was pushed along with the pieces of the broken wall."

Ⓐ fell down

Ⓑ shook

Ⓒ held

Ⓓ stayed

4. "The American government **developed** a system to warn people that tsunamis were coming."

CLUE: "They set up the Pacific Tsunami Warning System in Honolulu, Hawaii, to watch for events that could cause a tsunami."

Ⓐ created

Ⓑ grew

Ⓒ opposed

Ⓓ remembered

Facing Mother Nature's Wrath

Andrew Storms Miami

Sarah Beth Cavanah

At first, it seemed as if Hurricane Andrew would fizzle out. The first storm of the season was falling apart way out at sea.

[2] Andrew wasn't even expected to make it to land, let alone be strong enough to be a disaster.

[3] But things aren't always what they seem. Andrew didn't fizzle out. The storm gathered its strength and set a path for the city of Miami, on Florida's east coast.

[4] Andrew went from being a forgettable storm to the largest natural disaster ever to strike the United States.

A Strange Storm

[5] Andrew was a strange hurricane from the beginning.

[6] All hurricanes begin life as tropical storms. The storms are almost always born in the tropic zone of the globe. (That's why they are "tropical" storms.)

[7] The tropic zone is the area around the equator between the latitude lines of the Tropic of Cancer and the Tropic of Capricorn.

[8] Tropical storms form in this area over the Atlantic Ocean where it's very hot and very humid. And this is exactly what tropical storms love. They feed off the heat and moisture.

[9] If the conditions are right, the storms will grow strong enough to become hurricanes.

[10] Hurricanes are huge storms with winds that blow more than 74 miles per hour. Hurricanes are so large, they are actually many storms acting like a team. The storms organize themselves around the hurricane's center, called the "eye."

[11] But it looked as if Andrew would never get that strong. Andrew

was born outside the tropic zone. Not a good place to be for a newborn storm.

[12]Andrew didn't have enough heat and moisture to feed on. As the storm drifted toward the Florida coast, it started to die. Andrew's winds became weaker. The storm was also starting to break apart.

[13]It looked as if Andrew was a dud.

[14]But then something happened. The weather around Andrew started to change.

[15]Heat and moisture were pumped into the dying storm. Andrew ate it all up.

[16]The storm grew stronger off its new food. Andrew's winds started blowing harder. And then it headed for the coast.

Waiting for Andrew

[17]Andrew had gone from a dying storm to the strongest kind of hurricane. It had caused a lot of damage in the Bahama Islands off Florida's coast.

[18]Now it was heading straight for Miami.

[19]Officials asked the people of Miami to leave their homes. Hurricanes can be very dangerous.

So the officials wanted the people to go to safe places away from the storm.

[20]But many people didn't heed the warning. Miami gets a hurricane about every five years. People said they had made it through hurricanes before. They weren't scared of Andrew.

[21]But Miami hadn't seen a big hurricane for 25 years. And Miami had never seen a hurricane as strong as Andrew.

[22]The people of Miami nailed boards to their windows. They brought everything inside so it wouldn't blow away.

[23]Long lines formed at grocery stores. People were stocking up on food. They were also buying batteries and candles in case the electricity went out.

[24]On the night of August 23, meteorologists said Andrew was expected to hit Miami the next morning.

[25]After sunset, the usually busy streets of Miami were empty. People had either left town or were preparing for the storm inside their homes.

[26]But Andrew was a strange storm from the start. And the storm was going to arrive early.

Facing Mother Nature's Wrath

Andrew Comes Ashore

[27]By the time David Fisher went to bed it was raining very hard.

[28]David had tried to prepare his home as well as he could.

[29]He thought about opening the windows a little. He thought this might save them from being broken by the storm.

[30]Sometimes the air pressure outside a house drops very quickly before a hurricane hits. The pressure inside the house stays the same. The difference in the pressures can cause windows to break out from the inside. It's sort of like when you try to put too much air into a balloon, only backward.

[31]David decided to leave his windows closed. But he noticed the fans in the roof.

[32]David knew the fans could be ripped out by the storm. But it was too late. He decided to just go to bed. Whatever happened would happen.

[33]David was barely asleep when . . . Boom!

[34]David and his wife woke up quickly.

[35]"What was that?" David's wife asked.

[36]"I don't know," David said. When the sound didn't repeat, David decided something had hit the house.

[37]Hurricane Andrew had arrived.

[38]The danger in a hurricane isn't in the rain. The danger is in the wind.

[39]David was lucky. His fans didn't blow out in the storm. But one of his neighbors was less lucky. The loud crash David and his wife heard was the sound of a fan being blown into the side of their house. If it had been blown in a slightly different direction, it would have crashed through David's glass doors and hurt someone.

[40]The National Hurricane Center was not far from David's home. At the center, top American meteorologists track hurricanes for the entire country. But a hurricane had never hit the center dead-on.

[41]The center delivers reports on storms to television stations. That way, the stations can get the reports to all the people in the path of the storm.

[42]During the early morning hours of August 24, 1992, the National Hurricane Center was showing a radar report on the path of the storm. Suddenly, the screen went blank.

[43]The scared people of Miami waited for the picture to return. Outside, Hurricane Andrew was blowing harder than ever.

[44]A few tense moments passed.

[45]Then a television reporter came on screen. He explained that there would be no more reports from the National Hurricane Center. The wind had blown so hard, it had blown the radar equipment off the roof.

[46]Before that night, the scientists believed the center and its equipment could survive even the worst hurricane. But they had never expected a storm like Andrew.

Andrew's Aftermath

[47]In the morning, David Fisher came out from his home.

[48]The sky was gray. It was very strange. Miami is known for its sunny skies.

[49]David could also see where the fan had hit his house. The dent would always be a reminder of Andrew's fury.

[50]Other things were different too. Windows had been blown out of houses.

[51]But that wasn't all. David looked up and down the streets. Something was wrong.

[52]Then David realized what had changed. All the trees were gone. Andrew had been strong enough to

rip the trees out of the ground and carry them away.

[53] As terrible as Hurricane Andrew had been, David and his neighbors were lucky.

[54] Fifteen people had died during the storm. Thousands of people were suddenly homeless. Most of their homes were too damaged to be lived in. A few of the houses had just blown away.

[55] The fact that so many homes were destroyed surprised a lot of people. Miami had strict building rules. These rules were meant to make homes strong enough to survive storms like Andrew.

[56] But over the years builders had decided to save money by not following the rules. Their attempt to save money caused many people to lose their homes. Many people in Miami were very angry.

[57] Humans and their homes weren't the only things to be hurt during the storm. If all the trees and other debris were stacked together, they would be the same size as six Great Pyramids of Egypt.

[58] But Hurricane Andrew had positive effects, as well. The storm made beaches bigger. This gave endangered turtles more space to build their nests.

[59] Hurricane Andrew was also the first test of a new hurricane tracking method. This method can give people more warning about when a hurricane will hit. It also can better predict which way a hurricane will go.

[60] But when everything was added up, Hurricane Andrew was terrible. After the storm left Florida, it traveled across the Gulf of Mexico to Louisiana. The damage there wasn't as bad as in Miami. But added together, Hurricane Andrew became the worst natural disaster to ever hit the United States.

[61] And to think, Andrew almost didn't even survive to become a hurricane!

If you have been timing your reading speed for this story, record your time below.

_____ : _____

Minutes   Seconds

UNDERSTANDING THE MAIN IDEA

The following questions will demonstrate your understanding of what the story is about, or the *main idea*. Choose the best answer for each question.

1. This story is mainly about

Ⓐ how a storm just missed hitting Miami.

Ⓑ how a storm that was supposed to be bad turned out to be mild.

Ⓒ how Hurricane Andrew struck California.

Ⓓ how a storm no one was worried about turned into a huge disaster.

2. This story could have been titled

Ⓐ "Big Storm Is Really Small."

Ⓑ "Little Storm Grows Big."

Ⓒ "Andrew Misses Miami."

Ⓓ "A Few Drops of Rain."

3. Which detail best supports the main idea of this story?

Ⓐ People said they had made it through hurricanes before, and they weren't scared of Andrew.

Ⓑ Sometimes the air pressure outside a house drops very quickly before a hurricane hits.

Ⓒ Miami had strict building rules.

Ⓓ Hurricanes feed off heat and moisture.

4. Find another detail that supports the main idea of this story. Write it on the lines below.

_____

_____

RECALLING FACTS

The following questions will test how well you remember the facts in the story you just read. Choose the best answer for each question.

1. Almost all hurricanes start

Ⓐ over land.

Ⓑ in the tropic zone of the globe.

Ⓒ near the Earth's poles.

Ⓓ in the Pacific Ocean.

2. Before the storm, officials asked the people of Miami to

Ⓐ stay inside.

Ⓑ leave their homes.

Ⓒ rush to the beaches.

Ⓓ watch the television.

3. The loud sound David and his wife heard was

Ⓐ a tree being ripped out of the ground.

Ⓑ thunder.

Ⓒ a nearby house falling down.

Ⓓ a fan being blown into the side of their house.

4. After the storm, David realized that

Ⓐ all the neighborhood's trees were gone.

Ⓑ the sky was too sunny.

Ⓒ his neighbor's house was gone.

Ⓓ he should have left Miami.

Facing Mother Nature's Wrath

READING BETWEEN THE LINES

An *inference* is a conclusion drawn from facts. A *generalization* is a general statement, idea, or rule that is supported by facts. Analyze the story by choosing the best answer to each question below.

1. **What conclusion can you draw from paragraphs 8–9?**

   Ⓐ Hurricanes can form anywhere on Earth.

   Ⓑ Hurricanes usually form during winter.

   Ⓒ Hurricanes can become very strong feeding off cold water.

   Ⓓ Hurricanes need heat and moisture to become strong.

2. **What conclusion can you draw from paragraph 23?**

   Ⓐ The grocery store was having a special hurricane sale.

   Ⓑ People wanted to make sure they had enough food to last a few days.

   Ⓒ The grocery store's workers refused to come to work.

   Ⓓ The people were preparing for hurricane parties.

3. **What generalization can you make from this story?**

   Ⓐ Big hurricanes often catch cities off guard.

   Ⓑ Hurricanes always catch people by surprise.

   Ⓒ You can never be prepared for a hurricane.

   Ⓓ No one knew that Andrew was coming.

4. **It can be inferred from the story that**

   Ⓐ Miami had never seen a hurricane before.

   Ⓑ Miami needed to make many changes before the next hurricane.

   Ⓒ Miami could have survived an even stronger storm without damage.

   Ⓓ nothing good came out of Hurricane Andrew.

DETERMINING CAUSE AND EFFECT

Choose the best answers for the following questions to show the relationship between what happened in the story (*effects*) and why those things happened (*causes*).

1. Because Andrew was born outside the tropic zone,

Ⓐ it looked as if Andrew would never be strong.

Ⓑ it was a strong storm from the start.

Ⓒ the people of Miami knew the storm was coming their way.

Ⓓ it was moving twice as fast as other storms.

2. What happened because heat and moisture were pumped into Andrew?

Ⓐ Andrew changed direction and headed to Miami.

Ⓑ Andrew went from a strong storm to a weak storm.

Ⓒ Andrew went from a weak storm to a strong storm.

Ⓓ Andrew changed direction and missed Miami.

3. Why did David and his wife wake up during the night? Answer on the lines below, using complete sentences.

_____

_____

_____

_____

_____

4. Why did endangered turtles have more space to build their nests?

Ⓐ Hurricane Andrew made the beaches bigger.

Ⓑ Hurricane Andrew destroyed houses where the turtles nest.

Ⓒ Officials said people could no longer build houses on the beach.

Ⓓ The beach was turned into a state park.

———— ■ ————

USING CONTEXT CLUES

Skilled readers often find the meaning of unfamiliar words by using *context clues*. This means they study the way the words are used in the text. Use the context clues in the excerpts below to determine the meaning of each **bold-faced** word. Then choose the answer that best matches the meaning of the word.

1. "At first, it seemed as if Hurricane Andrew would **fizzle** out."

CLUE: "The first storm of the season was falling apart way out at sea."

- Ⓐ fake
- Ⓑ hide
- Ⓒ die
- Ⓓ sparkle

2. "But many people didn't **heed** the warning."

CLUE: "People said they had made it through hurricanes before. They weren't scared of Andrew."

- Ⓐ ignore
- Ⓑ follow
- Ⓒ understand
- Ⓓ like

3. "The dent would always be a reminder of Andrew's **fury**."

CLUE: "David could also see where the fan had hit his house."

- Ⓐ strength
- Ⓑ fun
- Ⓒ end
- Ⓓ forecasters

4. "Miami had **strict** building rules."

CLUE: "The fact that so many homes were destroyed surprised a lot of people. . . . These rules were meant to make homes strong enough to survive storms like Andrew."

- Ⓐ easy
- Ⓑ rigid
- Ⓒ lazy
- Ⓓ no

———— ▬ ————

The Red River Rampage

Jane Duden

The winter of 1996–1997 was brutal. It brought 98 inches of snow to the Midwest. That's twice as much as normal.

By April, eight blizzards had pounded western Minnesota and North Dakota. It was the worst winter anyone there had seen. Livestock froze. Farm buildings caved in. Whole towns shut down. Snow piled in 12-foot drifts.

Then came the snowmelt. Then came the flood.

One emergency official warned, "Yes, we're going to have floods. There is little we can do to stop the water. But we can be ready for it. And be sure that people are out of harm's way."

Were they ready? Three million dollars in emergency dikes and pumps could not stop the water. Sandbags by the millions were not nearly enough.

It was April 5, 1997, when the Minnesota River and the Red River of the North became paths of destruction. The floods would play out for a full month.

Until then, the Flood of 1970 had been everyone's worst memory in the Red River Valley. But it was about to be topped by the Flood of 1997. A flood like this happens only once in 500 years!

The Flood Begins

The floods began on April 5, 1997. The first cities to flood were Breckinridge, Montevideo, and Granite Falls in Minnesota.

In Breckinridge, Jack Thompson summed it up. "No one knew what a 500-year flood would be like. You just can't imagine 50 miles of water around you in every direction."

Throughout April, the Red River raged from Breckinridge to the

Canadian border. Towns on its banks filled up like bathtubs. Water swirled in the streets. It lapped at rooftops. It covered farms six miles from its banks. Dead cattle and all kinds of junk floated in it.

[11]On to Fargo it flowed and flooded. Then on to Grand Forks. The Red River had been rising more than two feet per day.

[12]The National Weather Service (NWS) watched around the clock. The NWS had raised its water peak, or crest, forecast five times in five days. Half of Grand Forks was flooded. All of East Grand Forks was flooded.

[13]The people fought the water. You could hear the fight day and night—the thunder of big trucks hauling clay and sandbags, the backup beeps of front loaders and bulldozers, the throbbing rotors of rescue helicopters, the constant howl of sirens, and the shouts of helpers filling sandbags. You could hear people hauling sandbags and people piling sandbags.

[14]On April 19, the river was 53 feet high. Grand Forks mayor Pat Owens had to tell thousands of people to give up the fight. Thousands of residents evacuated. The weary people let nature take its course.

[15]Everyone thought the worst had already happened. But the flood caused shorts in electrical wires. On April 19, the heart of Grand Forks went up in flames. Fire destroyed 11 buildings downtown. On April 20, the city's water supply ran out. And still the river rose.

[16]One man watched the water just before he left town. "It was really calm," he said. "It's like in normal times when you're sitting by the river. Except you see big trees floating by, pulled out by their roots. Then you look at the river with your mouth open."

[17]By April 20, Grand Forks and East Grand Forks were ghost towns. Nearly 60,000 people had left. The National Guard patrolled the streets, looking for stranded residents. The river would reach its peak the next day at 54.11 feet. That was more than 26 feet above flood stage.

[18]The only sound now was a gentle gurgle. It was the Red River running deep. Deep through the streets of Grand Forks on its North Dakota side. Deep through East Grand Forks on its Minnesota side.

North to Canada

[19]From Grand Forks, the flood moved on. It flowed north. It

swamped Ste. Agathe under six feet of water. The Flood of 1997 wouldn't really end until early May. That's when the crest of the Red River began mixing with the waters of Lake Winnipeg.

[20]More than 25,000 Manitobans had already been forced from their homes and farms. The floodwater drove out 8,000 Winnipeggers too. On May 1, Winnipeg, Canada, braced for the worst.

[21]Winnipeg had 76 miles of permanent dikes along its main rivers. The mayor gave orders to raise those so they could handle a break. The job required 1 million sandbags. And it took three days. The city also made temporary dikes with 5 million sandbags. Luckily,

they had the Red River Floodway. And the gates could be raised.

[22]The floodway was built in 1950 after a flood that covered much of Winnipeg. It takes overflow from the Red River around the city in a huge, human-made channel.

[23]In the end, the big ditch steered water around Winnipeg.

Fleeing the Flood in Grand Forks

[24]Where did flooded people go? They went to homes of friends or relatives and to homes of strangers. They went to Red Cross shelters in F-16 fighter jet hangars at Grand Forks Air Force Base and to college dormitories. (Classes were canceled for the rest of the term.) They went to anyplace dry.

[25]The news media became more important. Despite fire and flood, the *Grand Forks Herald* did not miss one edition. Hungry for news of their towns, evacuees read the *Herald*.

[26]Radio stations in Grand Forks and Fargo did everything to stay on the air through the crisis. Radio stations helped people find shelter. They helped family members find one another. They gave around-the-clock answers during call-in shows. People wanted news of their neighborhoods.

After the Flood

[27]The water went away, but the damage, grime, and mud did not. People came back to it. Everything had to be scrubbed with bleach. Houses had to be gutted. Soggy belongings had to be thrown out. Even muddy toys full of bacteria had to be trashed.

[28]Then came the rebuilding.

[29]Volunteers came from near and far. They came from all over the United States. They came from colleges, prisons, churches, the Red Cross, and the Salvation Army.

[30]Long lines of dump trucks hauled flood debris. During the busiest time, 120 trucks carried about 6 million pounds a day to the landfill.

[31]Air Force personnel, the National Guard, and the Army Corps of Engineers all helped. College and high school students who had helped sandbag the week before joined the cleanup.

[32]Red Cross trailers came with cleaning kits. They gave people coupons, or *vouchers*. These helped them buy clothes, food, medicine, and bedding.

[33]The Federal Emergency Management Agency (FEMA) sent rescue workers. FEMA gave out government money to help people rebuild. It sent trailers for people to live in while their homes were being fixed. Many residents lived in trailers for months. They called the trailers "FEMAville."

[34]People far from the flooded cities found ways to help. In Minneapolis and St. Paul, Minnesota, radio stations got together. They parked huge semitrailers. People could drop off supplies for the flood victims there.

[35]Adults shopped for food and supplies. Children shopped for toys. They came by the hundreds. They filled the trucks with their gifts.

[36]Karen Filloon, a weather forecaster with CBS/WCCO radio station in Minneapolis, helped with the project. She said, "When I went to schools to talk about the flood, kids worried about floods coming to their homes. They all wanted to help the flood victims. They went shopping to buy new toys to send."

[37]College students cared too. Many drove to the Red River Valley to help. They were told to get their shots and to wear clothes they could throw away because of the bacteria in cleanup sites.

[38]Grand Forks and East Grand Forks bought flood-wrecked houses. Then they tore them down. New parks and a $300 million dike system would take their place.

[39]The two cities wanted flood victims to stay. They gave money to people who built new homes in the city. They gave them land and low-interest loans. A year after the flood, 95 percent of those who had evacuated were back in Grand Forks.

[40]Reminders of the flood were everywhere. So sometimes it was hard to see the future. But community spirit held strong. People took control of their lives again. They cleaned. They rebuilt. Some even turned the flood into art.

[41]Students and teachers wrote and performed a musical based on the disaster. It was called *Keep the Faith*.

[42]The water ran deep at 54.11 feet. But it didn't match the depth of spirit. Grand Forks mayor Pat Owens spoke for everyone. "We will rebuild. And we will be stronger. And we will be in it together."

[43]President Bill Clinton came to see the flood damage. He talked about the valley's spirit and faith. He said, "Water cannot wash that away. Fire cannot burn that away. And a blizzard cannot freeze that away."

[44]The president was right.

If you have been timing your reading speed for this story, record your time below.

_____ : _____

Minutes   **Seconds**

UNDERSTANDING THE MAIN IDEA

The following questions will demonstrate your understanding of what the story is about, or the *main idea*. Choose the best answer for each question.

1. This story is mainly about

Ⓐ how a rainstorm flooded a city.

Ⓑ how cities in Minnesota, North Dakota, and Canada survived a flood.

Ⓒ how a snowstorm stopped a city.

Ⓓ how a newspaper kept publishing through a flood.

2. This story could have been titled

Ⓐ "Red River Drought."

Ⓑ "Red River Blizzard."

Ⓒ "Red River Flood."

Ⓓ "Red River Rodeo."

3. Which detail best supports the main idea of this story?

Ⓐ By April, eight blizzards had pounded western Minnesota and North Dakota.

Ⓑ College classes were canceled for the rest of the term.

Ⓒ Three million dollars in emergency dikes and pumps could not stop the water.

Ⓓ Radio stations in Grand Forks and Fargo tried to stay on the air.

4. Find another detail that supports the main idea of this story. Write it on the lines below.

_____

_____

RECALLING FACTS

The following questions will test how well you remember the facts in the story you just read. Choose the best answer for each question.

1. The first cities to be flooded were in

Ⓐ Minnesota.

Ⓑ Florida.

Ⓒ California.

Ⓓ Vermont.

2. When the river was 53 feet high, Grand Forks Mayor Pat Owens

Ⓐ asked the military to help fight the flood.

Ⓑ had to tell people to give up the fight against the flood.

Ⓒ declared the city a disaster area.

Ⓓ said the fight against the flood would go on.

3. In the end, Winnipeg was saved by

Ⓐ a big rainstorm.

Ⓑ the Red River Floodway.

Ⓒ the Canadian army.

Ⓓ a week without rain.

4. Volunteers came from all over the United States to

Ⓐ help rebuild the cities.

Ⓑ nurse the victims back to health.

Ⓒ open new stores in the area.

Ⓓ become radio announcers.

READING BETWEEN THE LINES

An *inference* is a conclusion drawn from facts. A *generalization* is a general statement, idea, or rule that is supported by facts. Analyze the story by choosing the best answer to each question below.

1. **What conclusion can you draw from paragraphs 2–3?**

   Ⓐ Minnesota usually has more than eight blizzards a year.

   Ⓑ The flood was caused by all the melted snow.

   Ⓒ It doesn't usually snow in Minnesota.

   Ⓓ The flood was caused by heavy rain.

2. **What conclusion can you draw from paragraph 13?**

   Ⓐ Most people thought they couldn't beat the flood.

   Ⓑ Only city workers helped fight the flood.

   Ⓒ Only a few people thought it was worth the effort to fight the flood.

   Ⓓ Many people were involved in fighting the flood in Grand Forks.

3. **What generalization can you make from this story?**

   Ⓐ Floods always cause millions of dollars in damage.

   Ⓑ Winnipeg was better prepared for the flood than some other cities.

   Ⓒ Sandbags are never very good at holding back flood waters.

   Ⓓ Floods only happen in Canada.

4. **It can be inferred from the story that**

   Ⓐ many people saw the flood as a chance to move to new cities.

   Ⓑ another flood won't happen in Grand Forks for 500 years.

   Ⓒ the people of Grand Forks didn't know what to do after the flood.

   Ⓓ the flood victims wanted to keep living in Grand Forks and rebuild it.

Facing Mother Nature's Wrath

DETERMINING
CAUSE AND EFFECT

Choose the best answers for the following questions to show the relationship between what happened in the story (*effects*) and why those things happened (*causes*).

1. Because the flood caused shorts in electrical wires,

Ⓐ a fire started in the heart of Grand Forks.

Ⓑ officials shut off electricity to the entire city.

Ⓒ the city was without electricity for months.

Ⓓ radio stations weren't able to keep running.

2. What happened because the flood covered so many homes in Grand Forks and East Grand Forks?

Ⓐ People had to move far away.

Ⓑ The cities had to be moved onto higher hills.

Ⓒ Other homes couldn't get running water.

Ⓓ The cities became ghost towns.

3. Why were college classes canceled for the rest of the term? Answer on the lines below, using complete sentences.

_____

_____

_____

_____

_____

4. Why were college students told to get shots and wear clothes they could throw away?

Ⓐ Officials were worried they would catch measles.

Ⓑ The water they were working in had bacteria in it.

Ⓒ So many clothes had been donated, officials didn't want them to go to waste.

Ⓓ Officials wanted to keep the clothes for a museum.

USING CONTEXT CLUES

Skilled readers often find the meaning of unfamiliar words by using *context clues*. This means they study the way the words are used in the text. Use the context clues in the excerpts below to determine the meaning of each **bold-faced** word. Then choose the answer that best matches the meaning of the word.

1. "The winter of 1996–1997 was **brutal**."

CLUE: "It brought 98 inches of snow to the Midwest. That's twice as much as normal."

  Ⓐ beautiful

  Ⓑ mild

  Ⓒ breathtaking

  Ⓓ horrible

2. "Thousands of residents **evacuated**."

CLUE: "Grand Forks mayor Pat Owens had to tell thousands of people to give up the fight."

  Ⓐ stayed

  Ⓑ exclaimed

  Ⓒ returned

  Ⓓ left

3. "On May 1, Winnipeg, Canada, **braced** for the worst."

CLUE: "More than 25,000 Manitobans had already been forced from their homes and farms. The floodwater drove out 8,000 Winnipeggers too."

  Ⓐ prepared

  Ⓑ held

  Ⓒ structured

  Ⓓ hoped

4. "Grand Forks and East Grand Forks bought flood-**wrecked** houses."

CLUE: "Then they tore them down."

  Ⓐ saved

  Ⓑ damaged

  Ⓒ escaped

  Ⓓ free

End-of-Unit Activities

1. What makes a natural disaster truly a "disaster"? Come up with your own degrees of disaster, such as "Mini Disaster" or "F-5 Disaster." The degrees should begin as the least severe and end as the most severe. Give each degree a name and list the criteria that define that degree. Then use your system to assign degrees of disaster to the natural disasters in this unit.

Degree Name:

Criteria:

Degree Name:

Criteria:

Degree Name:

Criteria:

Degree:

The Johnstown Flood _____

The Hilo and Aleutian Tsunami _____

Hurricane Andrew _____

The Red River Flood _____

End-of-Unit Activities

2. **Rank each of the stories in this unit, from the one you liked the most to the one you liked the least. For each story, write one interesting fact you learned. Then write a paragraph describing why you liked the story you ranked _1_ the best.**

LESSON 5 Ranking _____

_____

_____

_____

LESSON 6 Ranking _____

_____

_____

_____

LESSON 7 Ranking _____

_____

_____

_____

LESSON 8 Ranking _____

_____

_____

_____

Why did you like the story you ranked _1_ the best?

_____

_____

_____

_____

_____

Facing Mother Nature's Wrath

Words-Per-Minute Chart

Directions:

Use the chart to find your words-per-minute reading speed. Refer to the reading time you recorded at the end of each article. Find your reading time in seconds along the left-hand side of the chart or minutes and seconds along the right-hand side of the chart. Your words-per-minute score will be listed next to the time in the column below the appropriate lesson number.

No. of Words	Lesson 5 1,616	Lesson 6 1,163	Lesson 7 1,386	Lesson 8 1,465	Minutes and Seconds
80	1,212	872	1,040	1,099	1:20
100	970	698	832	879	1:40
120	808	582	693	733	2:00
140	693	498	594	628	2:20
160	606	436	520	549	2:40
180	539	388	462	488	3:00
200	485	349	416	440	3:20
220	441	317	378	400	3:40
240	404	291	347	366	4:00
260	373	268	320	338	4:20
280	346	249	297	314	4:40
300	323	233	277	293	5:00
320	303	218	260	275	5:20
340	285	205	245	259	5:40
360	269	194	231	244	6:00
380	255	184	219	231	6:20
400	242	174	208	220	6:40
420	231	166	198	209	7:00
440	220	159	189	200	7:20
460	211	152	181	191	7:40
480	202	145	173	183	8:00
500	194	140	166	176	8:20
520	186	134	160	169	8:40
540	180	129	154	163	9:00
560	173	125	149	157	9:20
580	167	120	143	152	9:40
600	162	116	139	147	10:00
620	156	113	134	142	10:20
640	152	109	130	137	10:40
660	147	106	126	133	11:00
680	143	103	122	129	11:20
700	139	100	119	126	11:40
720	135	97	116	122	12:00
740	131	94	112	119	12:20
760	128	92	109	116	12:40
780	124	89	107	113	13:00
800	121	87	104	110	13:20
820	118	85	101	107	13:40
840	115	83	99	105	14:00

Seconds

earth and sky

The Lost City of Pompeii

Sarah Beth Cavanah

The archaeologists knew they were uncovering an ancient city. They expected to find works of art. They expected to find pots and bowls and even toys. But they didn't expect to find people frozen in time.

[2]They found mothers and children huddled in corners of houses. They found men lying in the streets as if they had collapsed from running. The archaeologists even found people who looked like they were waiting quietly for death.

[3]But the people weren't real. They were shells of ash and rock nearly 2,000 years old. And they were victims of a horrible natural disaster. The people the archaeologists had found were the citizens of the ancient city of Pompeii. One summer day they all died when a volcano covered their city until it disappeared.

The City, the Sea, and the Volcano

[4]Almost 2,000 years ago, the people of Pompeii were thought to be some of the luckiest people in the world. They lived in a beautiful city by the sea. All around the city were peaceful farms and rich estates. Many citizens from the most powerful city in the world—Rome— owned property in Pompeii. They would visit often so they could enjoy relaxing vacations.

[5]Pompeii was also home to bakers and craftspeople, as well as merchants who owned ships that traveled the world bringing back exotic goods. And there were less fortunate people as well. Many of the people of Pompeii were slaves owned by the rich Roman nobles. They took care of the houses and worked the farms for their owners.

[6]It wasn't just the sea that made Pompeii beautiful. Just eight miles

from the city was Mount Vesuvius. The people of Pompeii knew Vesuvius had once been a volcano. They could tell from the rocks and land around the mountain. They also knew that Vesuvius had been dormant, or sleeping, for hundreds of years.

[7]Instead of fearing Vesuvius, the people of Pompeii thought of the volcano as a joyful place. Their legends said that the god of wine lived on top of the mountain. They thought the god held long parties where magical creatures would run through the green trees and flowers. No one in Pompeii could have guessed what was to come.

Pompeii Shakes

[8]Pompeii's peace was suddenly ended in the year 62 A.D. A terrible earthquake struck the town. Many of the beautiful rich estates crumbled to the ground. Inside the town, homes and shops were ruined.

[9]The earthquake wasn't the last. Every time the people of Pompeii would start to rebuild, another earthquake would strike. Pompeii would have to start all over again. Many of the rich Romans decided they could find better places to build vacation homes. They moved away. Pompeii was close to disappearing.

[10]But just before the once great city died, the people decided to make one more great push. They launched a big construction campaign to rebuild the city. The plan was to make Pompeii as great as it had been before the earthquakes started. Pompeii looked like a giant construction site.

[11]The plan was working. The people of Pompeii were proud to see their beautiful city restored. They covered their homes with beautiful murals showing the devastation of the earthquake and the beauty of what they had created.

[12]By August of the year 79 A.D., the project was almost completed. Pompeii was close to becoming the favorite vacation city for Romans. Even the emperor Julius Caesar's father-in-law lived on a Pompeii estate. No one knew why the earthquakes had started, but they were learning to live with them. Unfortunately, they were about to find out the earthquakes were just a sign of what was to come.

Vesuvius Awakens

[13]August 24 in the year 79 A.D. started as just another day. The people of Pompeii were going about their business as they always did. Suddenly, there was a huge

explosion. The ground shook, but this was different from the earthquakes that had become common.

[14]The explosion had come from peaceful Mount Vesuvius. A cloud shaped like a mushroom was forming over the top of the mountain. Vesuvius was no longer sleeping. The volcano had awakened.

[15]The people of Pompeii didn't know what to do. Vesuvius was a few miles away. They would have lots of time to outrun any lava from the volcano. But lava wasn't the problem. Immediately after the explosion, ash started to fall on the city. Soon rocks began falling from the sky. In an instant, Pompeii became a very dangerous place.

[16]The citizens of Pompeii started to flee. They headed for the shore. The sea was their only way out since Vesuvius blocked the inland roads. Soon, everyone was running for the sea.

[17]Pompeii was also on fire. The explosion and falling rocks knocked many lanterns to the ground. The

flames from the lanterns started fires in homes. They moved from house to house, scaring the already frightened people even more.

[18]Down at the shore, too many people were trying to get on too few boats. The owners of the ships took as many people as they could. They told the people left on land to wait until they could unload their passengers safely down the coast. Then they would come back with empty ships.

[19]For many, it was too long to wait. Thousands of people died waiting for the ships to return. Most died when Vesuvius released a large amount of toxic gas. The people died of suffocation as they huddled together waiting for a rescue.

The Forgotten City

[20]Vesuvius kept spitting out molten rock. In a week, the entire area around the volcano was covered with layers of ash and rock tens of feet deep. Pompeii and other cities were buried under these layers. The fertile green land had become a dead gray graveyard.

[21]For years, no one could live in the area. Slowly, the land recovered. After a while, grasses started to reclaim the area. Then young trees started to grow. People began to forget about the buried cities. They built new cities, new farms, and new estates.

[22]Time marched on. The Roman Empire fell. It was followed by a period known as the Middle (or Dark) Ages. Then came the Renaissance and the Age of Enlightenment. Scholars started to rediscover ancient Roman writings. Some even spoke about the city of Pompeii and the terrible fate its citizens had met.

[23]Explorers began looking for Pompeii and the other cities. They dug through the layers of dirt and volcanic ash. Many times they didn't find anything.

[24]Then in the 1700s, explorers dug into Pompeii. They have been digging there ever since. Pompeii has become one of the most famous archaeological sites in the world. It is a city frozen in time.

[25]The most famous features of Pompeii are the ash people. Pompeii was so quickly covered in ash that the bodies of Pompeii's people were trapped inside. The situation was much different than when a body is buried in the ground. The ash formed around the bodies. During the thousands of years since Vesuvius' eruption, the bodies slowly disintegrated.

[26]When archaeologists dug through the remains of the city, they found the empty holes where the bodies had been. They filled these holes with plaster. The holes worked like molds. When it was broken away, the plaster had formed the shape of a person.

[27]Some were just general shapes of people. Some were so detailed, they looked like statues of sleeping people, complete with hair. The molds of people showed the story of Pompeii in horrible detail. Archaeologists could see groups of people huddled together. They could see how people died, sometimes even the expressions on their faces.

[28]Archaeologists are still exploring Pompeii and the other victim cities of Vesuvius. They still find beautiful works of art, everyday tools, and children's toys. And they are also still finding the ash people. They are like ghosts living forever the day Vesuvius erupted.

If you have been timing your reading speed for this story, record your time below.

_____ : _____

Minutes   Seconds

Facing Mother Nature's Wrath

UNDERSTANDING THE MAIN IDEA

The following questions will demonstrate your understanding of what the story is about, or the *main idea*. Choose the best answer for each question.

1. This story is mainly about

Ⓐ an ancient city buried by a volcano.

Ⓑ a city destroyed by earthquakes.

Ⓒ a city destroyed by a flood.

Ⓓ an ancient city that was abandoned after a war.

2. This story could have been titled

Ⓐ "Burned to Death."

Ⓑ "Flood Claims Pompeii."

Ⓒ "Buried In Time."

Ⓓ "Escaping by Land."

3. Which detail best supports the main idea of this story?

Ⓐ Pompeii was so quickly covered in ash that the bodies of Pompeii's people were trapped inside.

Ⓑ All around Pompeii were peaceful farms and rich estates.

Ⓒ The Roman Empire fell.

Ⓓ No one knew why the earthquakes had started, but they were learning to live with them.

4. Find another detail that supports the main idea of this story. Write it on the lines below.

_____

_____

RECALLING FACTS

The following questions will test how well you remember the facts in the story you just read. Choose the best answer for each question.

1. In the remains of Pompeii, archaeologists found

Ⓐ the bodies of volcano victims.

Ⓑ the remains of Julius Caesar's father.

Ⓒ signs of extraterrestrial life.

Ⓓ shells of ash and rock nearly 2,000 years old.

2. In the year 62 A.D., Pompeii's peace was ended by a/an

Ⓐ volcano.

Ⓑ flood.

Ⓒ earthquake.

Ⓓ war.

3. Immediately after the explosion of Mount Vesuvius,

Ⓐ lava ran over the streets of Pompeii.

Ⓑ ash started to fall on Pompeii.

Ⓒ an earthquake shook the city.

Ⓓ all the ships sailed away.

4. During the Age of Enlightenment, scholars

Ⓐ forgot about the Roman Empire.

Ⓑ didn't want to disturb the city of Pompeii.

Ⓒ couldn't read Roman writings.

Ⓓ rediscovered Roman writings about Pompeii.

READING BETWEEN THE LINES

An *inference* is a conclusion drawn from facts. A *generalization* is a general statement, idea, or rule that is supported by facts. Analyze the story by choosing the best answer to each question below.

1. **What conclusion can you draw from paragraph 4?**

   Ⓐ Most people who lived in Pompeii were poor.

   Ⓑ Pompeii was thought to be a very good place to live.

   Ⓒ The people of Pompeii always won when gambling.

   Ⓓ Pompeii's weather wasn't very pleasant.

2. **What conclusion can you draw from paragraph 9?**

   Ⓐ The rich Romans left Pompeii because they knew the volcano would erupt.

   Ⓑ Even with the earthquakes, Pompeii was a busy, thriving city.

   Ⓒ The rich Romans left Pompeii because of the earthquakes.

   Ⓓ New people were moving to Pompeii all the time.

3. **What generalization can you make from this story?**

   Ⓐ People forgot about Pompeii because it wasn't interesting.

   Ⓑ Ash from volcanoes is often more dangerous than lava.

   Ⓒ Ancient cities were usually destroyed by volcanoes.

   Ⓓ Everyone who lived in Pompeii was rich.

4. **It can be inferred from this story that people go to Pompeii today to**

   _____

   _____

   _____

   _____

   _____

   ———— ▬ ————

Facing Mother Nature's Wrath

DETERMINING CAUSE AND EFFECT

Choose the best answers for the following questions to show the relationship between what happened in the story (*effects*) and why those things happened (*causes*).

1. Because the people of Pompeii thought the god of wine lived on Vesuvius,

Ⓐ they thought the mountain was a joyful place.

Ⓑ no one was allowed to go near the mountain.

Ⓒ they thought the mountain was a dangerous place.

Ⓓ they knew one day the mountain would destroy the city.

2. What happened because the city of Pompeii almost disappeared?

Ⓐ The emperor forced people to move to the city.

Ⓑ Earthquakes started to shake the city.

Ⓒ The people launched a great rebuilding campaign.

Ⓓ The people relocated to a place away from the volcano.

3. Why did the people flee toward the sea?

Ⓐ Boats were faster than walking on the road.

Ⓑ Officials told them they had to escape that way.

Ⓒ All the carts and carriages were buried by the ash.

Ⓓ Land escape routes were blocked by the volcano.

4. Why did explorers start looking for the lost city of Pompeii?

Ⓐ They thought there was great treasure buried with the city.

Ⓑ A new government said it would pay for archaeological digs.

Ⓒ They read about the city in ancient Roman writings.

Ⓓ They wanted to turn the city into a tourist attraction.

———— ■ ————

USING CONTEXT CLUES

Skilled readers often find the meaning of unfamiliar words by using *context clues*. This means they study the way the words are used in the text. Use the context clues in the excerpts below to determine the meaning of each **bold-faced** word. Then choose the answer that best matches the meaning of the word.

1. "The people the archaeologists had found were the citizens of the **ancient** city of Pompeii."

CLUE: "They were shells of ash and rock nearly 2,000 years old."

   Ⓐ awful

   Ⓑ nice

   Ⓒ new

   Ⓓ old

2. "Many of the beautiful rich estates **crumbled** to the ground."

CLUE: "A terrible earthquake struck the town."

   Ⓐ fell

   Ⓑ stuck

   Ⓒ ran

   Ⓓ skipped

3. "They launched a big construction **campaign** to rebuild the city."

CLUE: "The plan was to make Pompeii as great as it had been before the earthquakes started."

   Ⓐ election

   Ⓑ effort

   Ⓒ battle

   Ⓓ ship

4. "The most famous **features** of Pompeii are the ash people."

CLUE: "They [Archaeologists] still find beautiful works of art, everyday tools, and children's toys. And they are also still finding the ash people."

   Ⓐ survivors

   Ⓑ houses

   Ⓒ traits

   Ⓓ feats

The San Francisco Earthquake of 1906

Sarah Beth Cavanah

San Francisco police sergeant Jesse Cook was up early that morning. He worked for the great city of San Francisco, California. And Jesse could tell you, San Francisco had plenty for a policeman to do.

[2]In 1906, San Francisco was a hustling and bustling city of 400,000 people. San Francisco is much larger today, but in Jesse's time, it was still a young city. The oldest people in town could remember when Americans first came to California in large groups 60 years earlier. It was the great California Gold Rush of 1849.

[3]During the Gold Rush, little towns like San Francisco became great cities. After a while, the gold ran out. But most of the people stayed. The cities grew quickly. And as Jesse knew, fast-growing cities meant lots of crime. At the time, San Francisco was known as "the wickedest city in the world."

[4]Maybe that's why Jesse was up early that morning. San Francisco was a city that could keep a policeman on his toes. Jesse never knew what he would run into.

[5]On any given day, a policeman might be called to Chinatown, where Chinese immigrants often spoke little English. Or he could be called on to help solve a burglary of precious jewels. San Francisco was a major international place of business and trading. Or a policeman might have to break up a nighttime brawl at one of San Francisco's restaurants. The city was well known for great food, but it was also known for great fights.

[6]Just the night before, San Francisco's policemen helped make

sure an event went smoothly. The famous opera singer Enrico Caruso performed at the Grand Opera House. It was a great success. Everyone had gone to bed happy. In a place like San Francisco, who knew what tomorrow would bring!

The City Shakes

[7]Jesse Cook was ready for the day. Or at least he thought he was. The sun was just rising on April 18, 1906. It was going to be another beautiful California day.

[8]But instead of the usual quiet sounds of dawn, Jesse heard a low rumbling sound. Before he could even wonder what the sound could be, the ground started to shake.

[9]By now, Jesse knew what was going on. At first, Americans had to get used to California's earthquakes. There were usually a couple of minor earthquakes each year. The best thing was to just wait for the shaking to stop.

[10]But as Jesse waited for the ground to stop vibrating, he began to realize something was wrong. Instead of getting weaker, the shakes were getting stronger. Soon the ground was heaving. Jesse looked at the street. The earthquake was so strong, it looked as if the road were dancing!

[11]Finally, the shaking stopped. The buildings that had gone up so quickly had fallen just as fast. The quake had seemed to last forever, but it had really been just more than a minute.

[12]Since it was only a little after 5 a.m., the quake had woken most people from their sleep. The lucky ones didn't even know what had happened. The unlucky ones were in buildings that had fallen from the shake.

[13]It was horrible. But it wasn't over. The rumble started again. Then the shaking came, followed by the violent heaving that had already caused so much destruction. Again, the earthquake only lasted a little more than a minute. But this time, everyone in San Francisco was fully awake.

The Jewel in the Ring of Fire

[14]Back in 1906, there were lots of theories as to why earthquakes happened. What no one knew was that San Francisco—and all of California—was part of something scientists would later call the Ring of Fire.

[15]The Ring of Fire is really more of an oval. And it isn't made of fire either. The Ring of Fire is the name for the coastal areas surrounding the

Pacific Ocean. Some of these areas include Japan, Hawaii, South America, Alaska, and California.

[16]The "fire" comes from volcanoes. Many of the areas in the ring have the most active volcanoes in the world. But what do volcanoes have to do with earthquakes?

[17]Both earthquakes and volcanoes come from deep within the earth. Both are also often caused by the movement of the earth's plates.

[18]The earth is a lot like an orange. The top layer we live on is like the peel. Only the peel is in many pieces scientists call plates. Underneath the plates is a layer of hot, liquid rock. (When this rock is forced out of a volcano, it's called lava.)

[19]The earth's plates are very active. They float over the earth, but each plate moves in a different direction. Some are moving away from one another. Some are crashing into one another. They move too slowly for us to see, but over time, all that moving causes a lot of energy to build up where plates meet, called a fault line.

[20]California is one of the places where two plates are locked in a great battle. These two plates are pushing against each other. That's why California has so many earthquakes. But most weren't as strong as the one Jesse Cook survived. Scientists today estimate that it was one of the strongest earthquakes ever.

Dealing with Destruction

[21]Once the earthquake was over everything was still. Many thought the strange stillness was almost as spooky as the earthquake. But not everything was quiet. Crowded apartment buildings were on fire. Hotels had fallen down around the people inside. The city's gas plant exploded in a huge ball of fire.

[22]The jobs of police officers and firefighters were much different than they are today. There were no telephones for people to call and say where fires were. Then, firefighters had to pull the fire truck with horses. San Francisco's firefighters were very well trained. But the earthquake had destroyed the city's water pipes. There was no water to put out the fires!

[23]The fires were spreading to nearby buildings. Without water, firefighters didn't know what to do. Finally, they used dynamite to destroy buildings around the fire. They thought the fire wouldn't be able to spread if the buildings were gone.

[24]After one day, 250 city blocks were completely destroyed. The fires were still not out. They would last for three days. In the end, 514 city blocks were gone. The earthquake had claimed libraries, schools, restaurants, and almost all of Chinatown.

[25]Even today, no one is sure how many people died because of the earthquake. Newspapers of the time said 750 people. But historians today know that many more died, probably around 2,500 people. The extra people were foreign language speakers, women, and children who weren't on official lists of city residents.

[26]The disaster gave California a powerful lesson about safety. Because so many buildings were destroyed, buildings were made stronger. In time, the city was completely rebuilt.

[27]San Francisco has had many earthquakes since 1906, but none have been as bad. A very strong earthquake even stopped a World Series baseball game in 1996. The stronger buildings held up to the pressure, and many fewer people died. It was a hard lesson to learn, but thousands of lives have been saved.

If you have been timing your reading speed for this story, record your time below.

_____ : _____

Minutes   Seconds

UNDERSTANDING THE MAIN IDEA

The following questions will demonstrate your understanding of what the story is about, or the *main idea*. Choose the best answer for each question.

1. This story is mainly about

Ⓐ how an earthquake devastated San Diego.

Ⓑ how an earthquake devastated San Francisco.

Ⓒ how a policeman died in an earthquake.

Ⓓ how a policeman survived an earthquake.

2. This story could have been titled

Ⓐ "The Savior of Chinatown."

Ⓑ "San Francisco Shakes."

Ⓒ "Jesse's Very Good Day."

Ⓓ "Everyone Survives."

3. Which detail best supports the main idea of this story?

Ⓐ In 1906, San Francisco was a hustling and bustling city of 400,000 people.

Ⓑ The night before the earthquake, opera star Enrico Caruso performed.

Ⓒ The Ring of Fire is named after volcanoes.

Ⓓ After one day of fires caused by the earthquake, 250 city blocks were destroyed.

4. Find another detail that supports the main idea of this story. Write it on the lines below.

_____

_____

RECALLING FACTS

The following questions will test how well you remember the facts in the story you just read. Choose the best answer for each question.

1. In 1906, San Francisco was

Ⓐ a Mexican city.

Ⓑ the largest city in the world.

Ⓒ a very old city.

Ⓓ still a young city.

2. During the earthquake, Jesse thought the road looked like it was

Ⓐ still.

Ⓑ broken.

Ⓒ dancing.

Ⓓ gone.

3. One of the places in the Ring of Fire is

Ⓐ Africa.

Ⓑ California.

Ⓒ Europe.

Ⓓ Iowa.

4. In 1906, firefighters pulled fire trucks with

Ⓐ cars.

Ⓑ horses.

Ⓒ trucks.

Ⓓ manpower.

———— ■ ————

READING BETWEEN THE LINES

An *inference* is a conclusion drawn from facts. A *generalization* is a general statement, idea, or rule that is supported by facts. Analyze the story by choosing the best answer to each question below.

1. What conclusion can you draw from paragraph 1?

Ⓐ Jesse couldn't sleep that night.

Ⓑ San Francisco didn't have many policemen.

Ⓒ San Francisco was a calm city with little crime.

Ⓓ San Francisco was a wild city with lots of crime.

2. What conclusion can you draw from paragraph 9?

Ⓐ No one in San Francisco had felt an earthquake before.

Ⓑ The people of San Francisco were used to mild earthquakes.

Ⓒ Jesse thought a tornado was coming.

Ⓓ Earthquakes didn't happen in California until Americans moved there.

3. What generalization can you make about earthquakes from this story? Answer on the lines below, using complete sentences.

_____

_____

_____

_____

_____

4. It can be inferred from the story that

Ⓐ most of San Francisco was destroyed in the earthquake.

Ⓑ very little of San Francisco was destroyed in the earthquake.

Ⓒ San Francisco needed better firefighters.

Ⓓ most of the people of San Francisco lived in Chinatown.

—————■—————

DETERMINING CAUSE AND EFFECT

Choose the best answers for the following questions to show the relationship between what happened in the story (*effects*) and why those things happened (*causes*).

1. Because people flocked to California during the Gold Rush,

Ⓐ the amount of earthquakes increased.

Ⓑ cities like San Francisco grew quickly.

Ⓒ there weren't enough people in Eastern cities to keep factories going.

Ⓓ the amount of crime in the cities decreased.

2. What happened because of the earthquake's shaking?

Ⓐ Jesse lost his job as a policeman.

Ⓑ Many buildings fell down.

Ⓒ Many people weren't on official city lists.

Ⓓ Enrico Caruso performed at the Grand Opera House.

3. Why did the earthquake happen?

Ⓐ Two of the earth's plates pushed against each other.

Ⓑ The Gold Rush attracted many people to San Francisco.

Ⓒ San Francisco was a hustling, bustling city.

Ⓓ The city's gas plant exploded in a huge ball of fire.

4. Why did firefighters use dynamite to destroy buildings?

Ⓐ The buildings were too old for people to live in.

Ⓑ They wanted to build stronger buildings to resist earthquakes.

Ⓒ They thought it would stop the spread of the fire.

Ⓓ Many people had moved to San Francisco during the Gold Rush.

———■———

USING CONTEXT CLUES

Skilled readers often find the meaning of unfamiliar words by using *context clues*. This means they study the way the words are used in the text. Use the context clues in the excerpts below to determine the meaning of each **bold-faced** word. Then choose the answer that best matches the meaning of the word.

1. "Or a policeman might have to break up a nighttime **brawl** at one of San Francisco's restaurants."

CLUE: "The city was well known for great food, but it was also known for great fights."

   Ⓐ dance

   Ⓑ bowl

   Ⓒ disturbance

   Ⓓ jail

2. "There were usually a couple of **minor** earthquakes each year."

CLUE: "The best thing was to just wait for the shaking to stop."

   Ⓐ big

   Ⓑ small

   Ⓒ major

   Ⓓ surprise

3. "But as Jesse waited for the ground to stop **vibrating**, he began to realize something was wrong."

CLUE: "Instead of getting weaker, the shakes were getting stronger."

   Ⓐ moving

   Ⓑ tumbling

   Ⓒ sounding

   Ⓓ climbing

4. "Many thought the strange **stillness** was almost as spooky as the earthquake."

CLUE: "But not everything was quiet."

   Ⓐ noise

   Ⓑ turmoil

   Ⓒ vision

   Ⓓ silence

Facing Mother Nature's Wrath

The Dust Bowl

Sarah Beth Cavanah

The United States Congress had its hands full. The Great Depression had hit America hard. More than one-third of the people in America had lost their jobs. Out-of-work Americans stood in line for hours to get soup and bread from charity centers.

[2] Congress was always arguing about how to help the country and themselves. Many wealthy Americans, like members of Congress, had lost a lot of money when the stock market crashed in 1929.

[3] A new plan to help the country recover was proposed almost every day. And almost every day, the members of Congress would angrily argue that the plans didn't do enough for their home districts.

[4] But some members of Congress had even more worries. In the Great Plains—an area that ran from North Dakota to Texas—most people were farmers. The Great Depression had hit farming hard too. The amount of money farmers could get for their crops had gone down. Sometimes prices were so bad, it cost more money to raise the crop than the farmer could get for selling it. But these were the lucky ones.

[5] Thousands of farmers had no crops to sell. A terrible drought had taken over the Great Plains. The longer it went without rain, the drier the ground became. The wet, fertile soil of the plains turned into a dry, dead dust. When the strong winds of the Plains blew, the dust would lift off the ground.

[6] The Great Plains senators and representatives told the others about great dust storms that would cover entire towns. Not only were the Plains people suffering from a bad economy, they were also dying from sickness caused by breathing in the dust.

[7]The Great Plains Congress members argued that the people they represented needed more help than other Americans. Someone had to find out why the storms were happening. And more importantly, someone had to figure out how to make them stop.

[8]"Hogwash!" the other members of Congress called. They said the stories of the storms were exaggerated. Then they would go back to describing why their districts needed help.

[9]These arguments happened often. Then one day, while Congress was debating what was being called the Dust Bowl, they were called over to the window. On the horizon, they could see the darkest cloud most of them had ever seen.

[10]"What is it?" someone asked.

[11]But the Plains congressmen knew what it was. The dust storms had gotten so bad, they had traveled 1,500 miles to Washington, D.C. Congress was about to learn firsthand how bad the storms could be.

Desert, Breadbasket, and Desert Again

[12]The Dust Bowl of the 1930s didn't stay a mystery for long. The cause of the storms was the same as the people who were suffering from them: farmers.

[13]A hundred years earlier, the Great Plains had had another name: the Great American Desert. Ever since explorers had first come across the great area of flat land, they had seen the area as a wasteland.

[14]It wasn't because plants didn't grow there. Grasses grew so tall and so thick they looked like an ocean when the wind blew through them.

[15]But the area wasn't what American farmers were used to. First, much less rain fell there than in the East. Instead of clearing trees, farmers would have to clear off herds of large animals like buffalo.

[16]The ultimate disadvantage of the Plains, though, was its sod. Sod is a hard layer of dirt that sits on top of the looser soil farmers need to plant crops. Most farmers used plows to break up sod each year before they planted. But the Plains sod was so hard that the farmers' wooden plows would break instead of the soil.

[17]For many years, settlers passed the Great Plains by. They took wagon trains across it to get to the easier lands of California and Oregon. They never even thought about stopping.

[18]That all changed when the steel plow was invented. Suddenly farmers could break the hard Plains sod. The results were fantastic. After centuries of only growing grass, the soils were full of the nutrients crops need to grow.

[19]In the first part of the 20th century, the population of the Plains exploded. Farmers grew wheat, corn, and barley in huge fields. Business was great. Instead of being called the Great American Desert, Americans called the Great Plains "the country's breadbasket."

[20]But the farmers didn't realize what they had done. They had rapidly changed the Plains' ecosystem—all the plants and animals of an area and the connections between them.

[21]The Plains was actually very delicate. Over thousands of years, a system had developed. Grasses would grow tall. Wandering herds of animals would wander through, trimming the grass and moving on. In the winter, the grasses would cover the ground, keeping it in place. The wind could blow and blow, but the sod would stay right where it was.

[22]By the 1930s, everything had changed. The prairie grasses were gone. In their place were the row crops like corn and wheat. The large herds were gone too. They were killed off by farmers and others who didn't want to share the land with such hungry animals.

[23]In the fall, farmers would harvest their crops. The protective layer of vegetation and sod was gone.

[24]The only thing holding the soil down was water. Since it was wet,

the soil stuck together. This made it heavier, and the wind couldn't pick it up. But when the drought started, the soil's last defense was gone. The strong Plains winds started to pick up the soil and blow it for miles.

[25]Before long, there was so much dust in the air that it started to form huge storms. The storms could last for hours and cover entire towns. Not only could nothing grow, people had a hard time even breathing.

Dust Everywhere

[26]Opal Musselman was a teenager in Kansas during the Dust Bowl. Her father was a farmer, and Opal helped with her sisters. But then the dust started to cover the land.

[27]First the crops wouldn't grow. Then all the plants started to die. Finally, the land really did look like a desert.

[28]The dust made even ordinary, everyday things hard. Girls like Opal were often counted on to do many household chores. Doors and windows didn't always keep the dust out of homes. At first, families would sweep out and dust their houses after every storm. They would have to remove bucketfuls of dirt and dust!

[29]But after a while, many people gave up and let the dust take over the house. They would sleep in beds full of dirt. They would eat food that was full of dust. The dust was everywhere.

[30]Dust was also in everyone's clothes. People tried to wash their clothes. But as soon as they put them out to dry (this was before electric clothes dryers), the clothes would just get dusty again.

[31]All of these things made life hard, but it was nothing compared to what happened to Opal's father and many others like him. Dust was constantly in the air, so people were always breathing it in. Mr. Musselman's lungs were filled with dust. It caused him to become sick with something called dust pneumonia.

[32]The sickness made it hard for Mr. Musselman to breathe. The doctors couldn't help. They were seeing more and more cases like his. But there was still no cure. Opal's father died from the effects of dust pneumonia.

[33]Opal found herself the head of her family before she was even 20 years old. Like many others, Opal's family owed money to the bank. Without someone to work the farm, Opal didn't have money to pay

the bank its monthly payment. The bank took over the farm and forced Opal and her sisters to move.

[34]Opal went to work. She traded her housekeeping skills for shelter and food from people who still had enough for others. Instead of being a carefree student, Opal spent her teen years working hard to support her sisters.

[35]But she made it through. Others did too. However, it took a lot of changes before the Plains would stop being the Dust Bowl.

Recovery

[36]Opal Musselman was able to stay in Kansas. But thousands of people were forced to leave the Plains completely. Some of them went back to the East Coast, but many took everything they could and left for California and Oregon.

[37]The people who left thought they were going to better places where they could start over. But they soon found out that the Great Depression was everywhere in the United States. They weren't welcomed and sometimes weren't even allowed in some towns.

[38]The people who didn't leave faced challenges too. The crops were still not coming in, and the dust was still blowing. And many farmers thought the government was trying to tell them that they were to blame.

[39]President Franklin Roosevelt and Congress sent scientists and agricultural experts to the Plains. They went around telling farmers that the way they were farming was causing the dust to fly.

[40]The scientists said they could help the farmers if they were willing to change. The solution to the dust storms was conservation—actions that try to save the soil. They said that if farmers would plant rows of trees around their field, they could block the wind. Then not as much wind would hit the fields and less dust would get picked up.

[41]There were other things farmers could do to help too. They could plow less. If they left part of their harvested crops on the ground, they would help hold the soil together. It wouldn't solve everything immediately, but these changes would be a start.

[42]After a decade of dust storms and drought, the Plains finally saw a wet year. The dust storms ended, and farmers' fields were green again. The new conservation methods slowed down the loss of soil, but it still goes on today. Now the soil is

mainly lost through water instead of wind. Each year, farmers lose soil that floats down the rivers.

[43]About the same time, the Great Depression ended too. But it wasn't conservation that stopped it. Instead, it was World War II.

[44]Suddenly, the demand for American goods and food was much higher. Farmers got good prices for their crops again.

[45]The Great Plains became America's breadbasket again. But it is becoming a desert again. Most of the water farmers use to irrigate their fields comes from underground sources. These sources, called aquifers, are drying up from overuse.

[46]The climate is changing too. Parts of Oklahoma and Texas are getting less rain than they used to. They are becoming real deserts through a process called desertification. These kinds of changes will be harder to fix than the problems that led to the Dust Bowl.

[47]Hopefully, the people of the Great Plains will never see a dust storm again. But it will take help from everyone.

If you have been timing your reading speed for this story, record your time below.

_____ : _____

Minutes   **Seconds**

UNDERSTANDING THE MAIN IDEA

The following questions will demonstrate your understanding of what the story is about, or the *main idea*. Choose the best answer for each question.

1. This story is mainly about

- Ⓐ how changing an area's environment caused dust storms.
- Ⓑ how tornadoes caused dust storms.
- Ⓒ how the U.S. Congress was stopped by dust storms.
- Ⓓ how a girl survived dust storms by doing housework.

2. This story could have been titled

- Ⓐ "Dirt in the Skies."
- Ⓑ "A Bowl of Dirt."
- Ⓒ "Cleaning House."
- Ⓓ "The Desert Blooms."

3. Which detail best supports the main idea of this story?

- Ⓐ Thousands of farmers had no crops.
- Ⓑ The solution to the dust storms was conservation—actions that try to save the soil.
- Ⓒ In the first part of the 20th century, the population of the Plains exploded.
- Ⓓ The bank took over the farm and forced Opal Musselman and her sisters to move.

4. Find another detail that supports the main idea of this story. Write it on the lines below.

_____

_____

_____

RECALLING FACTS

The following questions will test how well you remember the facts in the story you just read. Choose the best answer for each question.

1. When the stock market crashed in 1929,

- Ⓐ many people lost a lot of money.
- Ⓑ many people moved to the Great Plains.
- Ⓒ farmers started planting trees to block the wind.
- Ⓓ farmers started using steel plows to break the sod.

2. Explorers called the Great Plains the

- Ⓐ Great American Wasteland.
- Ⓑ Great American Mountains.
- Ⓒ Great American Flatlands.
- Ⓓ Great American Desert.

3. After the drought started, there was so much dust in the air that

- Ⓐ Congress sent breathing masks to the people of the Plains.
- Ⓑ everyone was forced to move away.
- Ⓒ it started to form huge dust storms.
- Ⓓ rivers dried up.

4. Scientists told Plains farmers to

- Ⓐ plant rows of trees to block the wind.
- Ⓑ clear all the soil of vegetation.
- Ⓒ keep farming as usual.
- Ⓓ move and try farming new land.

An *inference* is a conclusion drawn from facts. A *generalization* is a general statement, idea, or rule that is supported by facts. Analyze the story by choosing the best answer to each question below.

1. What conclusion can you draw from paragraph 1?

Ⓐ Many people were poor during the Great Depression.

Ⓑ Many people were rich during the Great Depression.

Ⓒ The Great Depression was caused by Congress.

Ⓓ Standing in lines was a fun hobby during the Great Depression.

2. What conclusion can you draw from paragraph 33?

Ⓐ Opal had to take care of her family even though she wasn't an adult.

Ⓑ Opal didn't want to stay in her family's house.

Ⓒ The bank bought Opal's house but let her family live there.

Ⓓ The government took care of Opal's family after her father died.

3. What generalization can you make from this story?

Ⓐ Dust storms happen during every drought.

Ⓑ Conservation can't help solve environmental problems.

Ⓒ Changing an environment too fast can have dangerous effects.

Ⓓ Farmers should never grow crops on the Plains.

4. It can be inferred from the story that

Ⓐ scientists knew the dust storms of the Great Depression would happen.

Ⓑ dust storms could return to the Great Plains.

Ⓒ dust storms will never happen on the Great Plains again.

Ⓓ planting rows of trees to block the wind didn't work.

DETERMINING CAUSE AND EFFECT

Choose the best answers for the following questions to show the relationship between what happened in the story (*effects*) and why those things happened (*causes*).

1. Because the dust storms had gotten so bad,

Ⓐ the government moved everyone away from the Great Plains.

Ⓑ the United States joined World War II.

Ⓒ Opal and her family had to leave their farm.

Ⓓ they traveled 1,500 miles to Washington, D.C.

2. What happened because the Plains sod was so hard?

Ⓐ Many people settled on the Great Plains.

Ⓑ Huge forests grew on the Plains.

Ⓒ Explorers called the Plains the "Land of Sod."

Ⓓ Wooden plows would break.

3. Why did Opal's father get dust pneumonia?

Ⓐ He was a generally unhealthy person.

Ⓑ It was hard for him to breathe.

Ⓒ He constantly breathed in dust from the air.

Ⓓ He smoked too much.

4. Why did the Great Depression end?

Ⓐ Farmers started plowing the land less.

Ⓑ The stock market crashed in 1929.

Ⓒ People found new homes away from the Great Plains.

Ⓓ America entered World War II, and demand for goods became high again.

———— ■ ————

USING CONTEXT CLUES

Skilled readers often find the meaning of unfamiliar words by using *context clues*. This means they study the way the words are used in the text. Use the context clues in the excerpts below to determine the meaning of each **bold-faced** word. Then choose the answer that best matches the meaning of the word.

1. "A new plan to help the country recover was **proposed** almost every day."

CLUE: "And almost every day, the members of Congress would angrily argue that the plans didn't do enough for their home districts."

   Ⓐ taken

   Ⓑ offered

   Ⓒ written

   Ⓓ shot

2. "The **ultimate** disadvantage of the Plains, though, was its sod."

CLUE: "But the Plains sod was so hard that the farmers' wooden plows would break instead of the soil."

   Ⓐ smallest

   Ⓑ biggest

   Ⓒ usual

   Ⓓ littlest

3. "But when the drought started, the soil's last **defense** was gone." (paragraph 24)

Write what you think the **bold-faced** word means. Then record the context clues that led you to this definition.

Meaning:

_____

_____

_____

Context clues:

_____

_____

_____

4. "Instead of being a **carefree** student, Opal spent her teen years working hard to support her sisters."

CLUE: "Opal went to work. She traded her housekeeping skills for shelter and food from people who still had enough for others."

   Ⓐ careless

   Ⓑ slow

   Ⓒ happy

   Ⓓ serious

The Biggest Tornado Ever— Oh, Yeah, 44 Others Too

Sarah Beth Cavanah

May 3, 1999, started off as just another late spring day in Oklahoma City. Kids headed off to school. Their parents headed off to work. The television weather forecasters said everyone was in for a great day. It would be nice and warm, with just a small chance of storms that afternoon.

[2]They couldn't have been any more wrong. May 3, 1999, would go down in Oklahoma history. It would go down in meteorological history, as well. There would be storms that afternoon. And those storms would produce the biggest tornado ever recorded.

[3]That tornado would be just one of 45 tornadoes to attack Oklahoma and Kansas before the night was over.

Moderate Chance of Storms

[4]By the time the noon newscasts came on, the weather forecasters had upgraded the chance of storms. Now, they said, there was a moderate chance of an afternoon storm or two.

[5]But at the University of Oklahoma, meteorology professor Howard Bluestein was beginning to wonder. Professor Bluestein is a tornado expert. He leads a team of tornado chasers, students and teachers who try to follow storms to collect scientific information on them. Professor Bluestein and his students were even the inspiration for the 1995 blockbuster movie "Twister."

[6]Professor Bluestein looked at all the information available on the day's weather. "Conditions look right," he told his team. They broke up into smaller groups and headed

out in their white vans loaded with scientific measuring equipment.

[7]But to everyone else on the University of Oklahoma's campus, it was just another day. Even as the skies started to darken that afternoon, most students were still more concerned about taking their final exams than some little storm.

[8]After all, storms and Oklahoma go together like peanut butter and jelly. Tornadoes were just part of life. Spring wasn't spring without at least one big storm.

[9]So even when a tornado warning was issued at 4:30 that afternoon, nobody really paid attention. Tornado warnings are even more common in Oklahoma than tornadoes. Unless one is coming their way, most people just keep on with what they're doing. But Oklahomans are experts on tornadoes. It wasn't long before they could tell something was wrong.

Outbreak

[10]Something was very wrong. High in the sky, a war and a race were going on. Summer was coming, and with it, warm air was pushing north from the Gulf of Mexico. This warm, wet air was pushing against the leftover cold air from winter. Of course, summer would eventually win—it always does.

[11]But the battle leads to tornadoes in an area of the United States called Tornado Alley. This Alley stretches up from Texas to Nebraska and then back down to Missouri. But Oklahoma is the busiest place on the Alley.

[12]That afternoon, the battle between warm and cold air was producing a race. High above the ground, strong winds were blowing very quickly. Closer to the ground, slower winds were trying to keep up. When the difference between the fast winds and slow winds gets to a certain level, they stop blowing in a straight line. Instead, the winds roll over each other, like a wheel on a car.

[13]If these rolling winds happen in the same place as a thunderstorm, a tornado can appear. Winds in a thunderstorm can blow straight up and down. These winds can tilt the other winds that were blowing like a wheel. The wheel turns on its side and reaches down to earth. A tornado is born.

[14]This process was going on all over Oklahoma on May 3. In Lawton, Oklahoma, police officer Don McGee was just finishing his day of work. Officer McGee was heading off to his second job when he noticed the sky. It was dark gray and churning. He could see a wall

Facing Mother Nature's Wrath

cloud, a very tall cloud where tornadoes form.

[15]Little tails were coming out from the wall cloud. Officer McGee pulled over with other people to watch. These were going to be tornadoes big enough to do damage, but not huge. All over Oklahoma, small tornadoes were forming. There were so many, it would take a couple of days for experts to determine the exact number. But near Chickasha, Oklahoma, the biggest tornado ever was forming.

F-5

[16]Television crews were having trouble keeping up with all the storms. Tornadoes kept sprouting up all over the state. Which ones should they chase?

[17]But as the day was beginning to end, tornado whistles started to scream in Chickasha, Oklahoma. A tornado was on the ground, and it was growing. The tornado was moving slowly. That wasn't a good sign. This tornado had strength and power. Worst of all, it was headed straight for the heavily populated areas of Oklahoma City.

[18]By now, everyone was taking this storm very seriously. Tornadoes are judged on a scale, sort of like earthquakes. Most tornadoes are F-1s and F-2s. These are small tornadoes

with slower wind speeds. F-3s and F-4s are more serious. These tornadoes could get to be hundreds of feet across with very strong winds.

[19]The tornado that was headed for Oklahoma City was much worse. It was an F-5, the biggest category of tornado. It was a mile wide and had winds traveling 318 miles per hour. These are the fastest winds ever recorded on the entire planet. Anything that got in the way of this storm didn't stand a chance.

Total Destruction

[20]Hundreds of thousands of people were in the path of the storm. Families tried to find the best shelter they could. Many houses in Oklahoma don't have basements or storm shelters. So many people hid in closets or bathrooms holding mattresses over their bodies. A mattress can protect a person from falling and flying objects such as television sets and even couches.

[21]Nearly two hours after Oklahoma City residents were told the Chickasha tornado was headed their way, the funnel reached the suburb of Moore, Oklahoma. The mile-wide funnel ripped through Moore and crossed I-35 into Oklahoma City and Midwest City.

[22]Oklahoma City Police Captain Charles Allen saw the tornado move through the city. "I thought to myself, 'There's no way something that big moves on this earth.' " Darkness had fallen. It covered the sad scene the tornado left behind. Entire neighborhoods were gone. No houses. No cars. No trees. Nothing.

[23]Even as the biggest tornado was moving away from the city and growing smaller, other tornadoes were springing up. A tornado was threatening to destroy all of Bridge Creek, Oklahoma.

[24]A boy and his mother ran out of their house to hide in a creek. Grady County Deputy Bob Paul would later talk to the six-year-old boy. The boy had seen his mother picked up and carried away by the wind. "When [rescue workers] found him, he was wandering the road," Deputy Paul said. Eleven people in Bridge Creek died in the tornado, and most of the town was destroyed.

[25]Later that night, another big tornado bit into the Wichita, Kansas, area. Steve Atherton didn't have enough time to get his three youngest children out of their mobile home. The lights flickered as the tornado knocked down power lines.

[26]Then Atherton could hear the noise. Many tornado survivors say a tornado sounds like a freight train coming right at you. But Atherton thought it sounded like millions of bees swarming around his home.

[27]Steve rushed his children into the laundry room just in time. The tornado was there. Its force knocked over the washer and dryer onto Steve. Even though he wasn't a large man, Steve was able to hold both the washer and dryer from falling on his children until the storm passed.

Aftermath

[28]Morning finally came. Instead of bringing relief, the morning light just revealed how terrible the night's storms had been. Thousands of people were homeless. Forty-five tornadoes had claimed the lives of 43 people, from toddlers to elderly people. Oklahoma looked like it had been through a whole war in just one night.

[29]Rescue workers dug through

fallen-down houses to look for survivors trapped in rubble. Because of safety concerns, people weren't allowed to see what was left of their homes. Later, they would find out that not much was left.

[30]When Midwest City resident Christy Smith was finally let back into her neighborhood, she had trouble finding her house. Without houses, trees, signs and even some roads, how can you tell where your home is?

[31]"When we got here," Smith told a reporter at her home, "I could only tell it was our house because of the bushes."

[32]It was terrible, and many people felt it was unfair. Just four years before, 168 people were killed when a terrorist bombed a building in downtown Oklahoma City. Another tragedy seemed like it would almost be too much.

[33]But Oklahomans knew they could handle the tornado because they had handled tragedy before. Students at the University of Oklahoma, which had not been hit by a tornado, stood in line for two hours to donate blood to help people hurt in the storms.

[34]The large lawn of a local television station became a collection place for donations of food, clothing, and other materials. Cars lined up for miles to drop off their donations. Before the end of the day, the lawn was filled with donations from people lucky enough not to have lost everything in the storm.

[35]Collections were also taking place across the country. All sorts of towns sent semitrailer trucks filled with donations to Oklahoma City. So much was collected that some of the trucks had to be diverted to Wichita, where there was more need.

[36]The recovery just kept on going. Hundreds of volunteers helped rebuild a neighborhood in Moore that had been destroyed. The volunteers were with Habitat for Humanity. Many of them had never done any construction before, but together, they rebuilt nearly 100 homes.

[37]Scientists, like Professor Bluestein, also managed to get something from the storm. The information they collected has helped them make better computer models. These models can help forecasters make better predictions.

If you have been timing your reading speed for this story, record your time below.

_____ : _____

Minutes　　**Seconds**

Facing Mother Nature's Wrath

UNDERSTANDING THE MAIN IDEA

The following questions will demonstrate your understanding of what the story is about, or the *main idea*. Choose the best answer for each question.

1. This story is mainly about

Ⓐ 44 days of tornadoes in Kansas and Missouri.

Ⓑ how the biggest tornado ever destroyed Houston, Texas.

Ⓒ an outbreak of tornadoes in Oklahoma and Kansas.

Ⓓ how a boy lost his mother in a tornado.

2. This story could have been titled

Ⓐ "Flood Watch."

Ⓑ "Chance of Snow."

Ⓒ "Winter Storm Watch."

Ⓓ "Tornado Warning."

3. Which detail best supports the main idea of this story?

Ⓐ By the time the noon newscasts came on, the weather forecasters had upgraded the chance of storms.

Ⓑ Professor Bluestein is a tornado expert.

Ⓒ Most tornadoes are F-1s or F-2s.

Ⓓ Forty-five tornadoes had claimed the lives of 43 people, from toddlers to elderly people.

4. Find another detail that supports the main idea of this story. Write it on the lines below.

_____

_____

RECALLING FACTS

The following questions will test how well you remember the facts in the story you just read. Choose the best answer for each question.

1. On the morning of May 3, 1999, weather forecasters said there

Ⓐ would be a tornado that afternoon.

Ⓑ was a strong chance of afternoon storms.

Ⓒ was no chance of afternoon storms.

Ⓓ was a slight chance of afternoon storms.

2. The area that stretches from Texas to Nebraska and back to Missouri is called

Ⓐ Storm Street.

Ⓑ Snow Strip.

Ⓒ Flood Lane.

Ⓓ Tornado Alley.

3. The worst and biggest category of tornadoes is called

Ⓐ A-1.

Ⓑ C-7.

Ⓒ Z-0.

Ⓓ F-5.

4. Because of safety concerns, after the tornado,

Ⓐ people weren't allowed back to their houses.

Ⓑ everyone in Oklahoma was asked to go to shelters.

Ⓒ many homes were demolished.

Ⓓ all schools were closed for the rest of the year.

READING BETWEEN THE LINES

An *inference* is a conclusion drawn from facts. A *generalization* is a general statement, idea, or rule that is supported by facts. Analyze the story by choosing the best answer to each question below.

1. **What conclusion can you draw from paragraph 6?**

   Ⓐ Professor Bluestein believed the weather forecasters were right.

   Ⓑ Professor Bluestein thought a tornado could form.

   Ⓒ Professor Bluestein was sending everyone home.

   Ⓓ Professor Bluestein didn't think a tornado would happen that day.

2. **What conclusion can you draw from paragraph 15?**

   Ⓐ The people watching the sky wanted to see the tornado form.

   Ⓑ The people watching the sky were looking at stars.

   Ⓒ The people watching the sky didn't know what was going on.

   Ⓓ The people watching the sky were part of a storm club.

3. **What generalization can you make from this story?**

   Ⓐ Most tornadoes are more than a mile wide.

   Ⓑ It is unusual for a tornado to be as big as the one that hit Moore, Oklahoma.

   Ⓒ No Oklahomans are used to living through tornadoes.

   Ⓓ Tornado victims never get much help after storms.

4. **It can be inferred from this story that people across the country**

   _____

   _____

   _____

   _____

   _____

   ⎯⎯ ▬ ⎯⎯

DETERMINING CAUSE AND EFFECT

Choose the best answers for the following questions to show the relationship between what happened in the story (*effects*) and why those things happened (*causes*).

1. Because Oklahomans are used to tornadoes,

  Ⓐ they don't have many storm shelters.

  Ⓑ everyone panicked when the tornado warning was put out.

  Ⓒ no one was really worried when a tornado warning was put out.

  Ⓓ they often have to rebuild entire neighborhoods.

2. What happened because winds in the storm were blowing at different speeds?

  Ⓐ They canceled each other out, and the storm passed.

  Ⓑ The winds started rolling over each other like a wheel.

  Ⓒ Everyone could see that a tornado was coming.

  Ⓓ All the tornadoes stopped.

3. Why did people put mattresses over their bodies during the storm?

  Ⓐ Mattresses can protect people in a storm from flying objects like televisions.

  Ⓑ They were superstitious about tornadoes.

  Ⓒ Having heavy mattresses on them would keep them from flying away with the storm.

  Ⓓ The mattresses kept them from getting wet.

4. Why did Christy Smith have a hard time finding her house?

  Ⓐ She had been hit on the head and had some memory loss.

  Ⓑ Her house had been moved to a new neighborhood.

  Ⓒ Police wouldn't let her back into her neighborhood.

  Ⓓ There were no standing houses, trees, signs, or roads to tell her where she was.

———■———

USING CONTEXT CLUES

Skilled readers often find the meaning of unfamiliar words by using *context clues*. This means they study the way the words are used in the text. Use the context clues in the excerpts below to determine the meaning of each **bold-faced** word. Then choose the answer that best matches the meaning of the word.

1. "And those storms would **produce** the biggest tornado ever recorded."

CLUE: "There would be storms that afternoon."

Ⓐ stop

Ⓑ kill

Ⓒ make

Ⓓ push

2. "Officer McGee was heading off to his second job when he **noticed** the sky."

CLUE: "He could see a wall cloud, a very tall cloud where tornadoes form."

Ⓐ ignored

Ⓑ looked at

Ⓒ practiced

Ⓓ drew

3. "Tornadoes are **judged** on a scale, sort of like earthquakes."

CLUE: "Most tornadoes are F-1s and F-2s. These are small tornadoes with slower wind speeds."

Ⓐ measured

Ⓑ found

Ⓒ criticized

Ⓓ formed

4. "Forty-five tornadoes had **claimed** the lives of 43 people, from toddlers to elderly people."

CLUE: "Rescue workers dug through fallen-down houses to look for survivors trapped in rubble."

Ⓐ caused

Ⓑ taken

Ⓒ accepted

Ⓓ talked

End-of-Unit Activities

1. This unit, "Earth and Sky," contains four stories of disasters full of
   similarities and differences. Choose two disasters from this unit. In the Venn
   diagram below, compare and contrast those disasters. Record similarities in
   the part of the circles that overlaps, and differences in the individual circles.
   List at least five similarities and five differences.

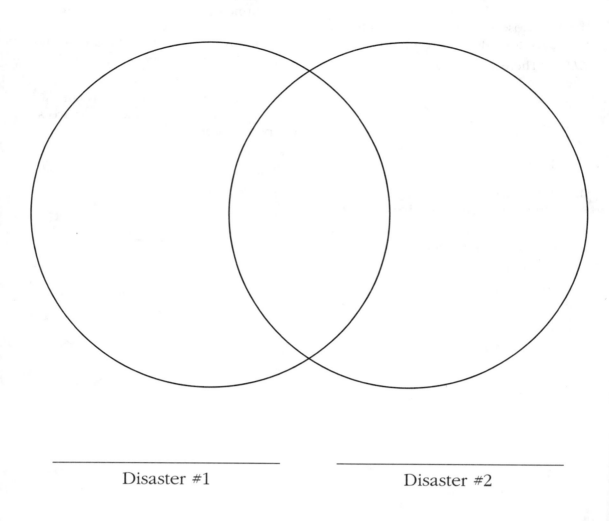

| Disaster #1 | Disaster #2 |

End-of-Unit Activities

2. **Rank each of the stories in this unit, from the one you liked the most to the one you liked the least. For each story, write one interesting fact you learned. Then write a paragraph describing why you liked the story you ranked *1* the best.**

LESSON 9 Ranking _____

_____

_____

_____

LESSON 10 Ranking _____

_____

_____

_____

LESSON 11 Ranking _____

_____

_____

_____

LESSON 12 Ranking _____

_____

_____

_____

Why did you like the story you ranked *1* the best?

_____

_____

_____

_____

_____

Directions:

Use the chart to find your words-per-minute reading speed. Refer to the reading time you recorded at the end of each article. Find your reading time in seconds along the left-hand side of the chart or minutes and seconds along the right-hand side of the chart. Your words-per-minute score will be listed next to the time in the column below the appropriate lesson number.

No. of Words	Lesson 9 1,317	Lesson 10 1,213	Lesson 11 1,826	Lesson 12 1,716	Minutes and Seconds
80	988	910	1,370	1,287	1:20
100	790	728	1,096	1,030	1:40
120	659	607	913	858	2:00
140	564	520	783	735	2:20
160	494	455	685	644	2:40
180	439	404	609	572	3:00
200	395	364	548	515	3:20
220	359	331	498	468	3:40
240	329	303	457	429	4:00
260	304	280	421	396	4:20
280	282	260	391	368	4:40
300	263	243	365	343	5:00
320	247	227	342	322	5:20
340	232	214	322	303	5:40
360	220	202	304	286	6:00
380	208	192	288	271	6:20
400	198	182	274	257	6:40
420	188	173	261	245	7:00
440	180	165	249	234	7:20
460	172	158	238	224	7:40
480	165	152	228	215	8:00
500	158	146	219	206	8:20
520	152	140	211	198	8:40
540	146	135	203	191	9:00
560	141	130	196	184	9:20
580	136	125	189	178	9:40
600	132	121	183	172	10:00
620	127	117	177	166	10:20
640	123	114	171	161	10:40
660	120	110	166	156	11:00
680	116	107	161	151	11:20
700	113	104	157	147	11:40
720	110	101	152	143	12:00
740	107	98	148	139	12:20
760	104	96	144	135	12:40
780	101	93	140	132	13:00
800	99	91	137	129	13:20
820	96	89	134	126	13:40
840	94	87	130	123	14:00

Seconds